The Urban Book Series

The Urban Book Series is a resource for urban studies and geography research worldwide. It provides a unique and innovative resource for the latest developments in the field, nurturing a comprehensive and encompassing publication venue for urban studies, urban geography, planning and regional development.

The series publishes peer-reviewed volumes related to urbanization, sustainability, urban environments, sustainable urbanism, governance, globalization, urban and sustainable development, spatial and area studies, urban management, transport systems, urban infrastructure, urban dynamics, green cities and urban landscapes. It also invites research which documents urbanization processes and urban dynamics on a national, regional and local level, welcoming case studies, as well as comparative and applied research.

The series will appeal to urbanists, geographers, planners, engineers, architects, policy makers, and to all of those interested in a wide-ranging overview of contemporary urban studies and innovations in the field. It accepts monographs, edited volumes and textbooks.

Indexed by Scopus.

Ninik Suhartini · Paul Jones

Beyond the Informal

Understanding Self-organized Kampungs
in Indonesia

Springer

Ninik Suhartini
School of Architecture
Design and Policy Development
Institut Teknologi Bandung
Bandung, Indonesia

Paul Jones
School of Architecture
Planning and Policy Development
Institut Teknologi Bandung
Bandung, Indonesia

ISSN 2365-757X   ISSN 2365-7588 (electronic)
The Urban Book Series
ISBN 978-3-031-22238-2   ISBN 978-3-031-22239-9 (eBook)
https://doi.org/10.1007/978-3-031-22239-9

This Springer imprint is published by the registered company Springer Nature Switzerland AG
The registered company address is: Gewerbestrasse 11, 6330 Cham, Switzerland

Foreword

According to the United Nations' newest publication on urbanization (UNDESA 2019) *World Urbanization Prospects*, Indonesia has been among the world's most rapidly urbanizing country in the past few decades. Indonesia is now home to more than 270 million people. Between 1980 and 2020, Indonesia's urban population grew about fivefold, from 32.8 to 152.9 million people. Rapid urbanization in Indonesian cities has produced an urban crisis marked by inadequate infrastructure, particularly housing.

Informality has been a distinct feature of cities of the Global South, including Indonesian cities. Urban informality is considered the norm rather than the exception. Some planning theorists (Porter 2011; Roy 2005; Yiftachel 2009) suggest that urban informality is not separable from urban formality. Urban informality should be seen as a system of norms governing transformation in cities of the Global South. Urban informality is a mode of urban transformation in the Global South. The state and planning in the Global South contribute to the production and maintenance of urban informality. Urban informality presents challenges and paradoxes for planners in the Global South.

Beyond the Informal: Understanding Self-Organized Kampungs in Indonesia carefully demonstrates that urban informality through informal socioeconomic activities in kampungs or informal settlements is the core feature of the urban transformation in Indonesian cities. Formal planning regulations and policies have little impact on residents of kampungs, who are primarily poor and disadvantaged. Kampung residents are often excluded from the benefits and opportunities received by other residents in the city. Jones and Suhartini brilliantly describe how kampung residents sustain their lives through self-organization practices. Kampungs or informal settlements in Indonesian cities are seen as self-organizing entities. Urban informality is visibly shown in spontaneous housing and associated spatial patterns built at the individual or group level in kampungs. After reading this important book, readers will come to realize that kampungs have a special place in the Indonesian urban fabric.

Planners in the Global South learned from their past experiences with slum clearance programs. They see that slum clearance programs only moved substandard houses to new places, particularly peripheral urban areas. A high level of household displacement has been one of the disappointing features of upgrading housing settlements. There was no need to demolish slums because they were part of the solution. This book uses the cases of kampungs in three major Indonesian cities: Kampung Marlina in Jakarta, Kampung Lebak Siliwangi in Bandung, and Kampung Pakualaman in Yogyakarta. The selection of these case studies is commendable. They are representative of the complexity and diversity of Indonesia's kampungs. These three kampungs have a distinctive history, combined with the diverse socioeconomic characteristics of their residents, governance systems, morphological evolution, interface typology, and adaptation strategies.

Using these three kampungs as their case studies, Jones and Suhartini provide a comprehensive framework that enables the reader to understand how the 'self-organize' approach is the solution in kampungs or informal settlements of Indonesian cities. The 'self-organize' approach is superior to total redevelopment in terms of affordability, flexibility, and encouraging human creativity in seeking value in life. In this approach, kampung residents improved their housing incrementally by using better materials and adding more space. The concept of self-organization is an essential element in understanding and explaining the urban development process, particularly in cities of the Global South. *Beyond the Informal* also defines key features of self-organization and new ways of looking at informality in kampungs, including historical socioeconomic drivers and development setting, autonomous agents, spatial units, complexity, feedback loops, self-governance, layers of governance, coevolution, rules and regulations, use of protocols, temporal dimensions, and physical diversity and spatial heterogeneity.

No scholar better captures the meaning and significance of kampung in the Indonesian urban fabric than Paul Jones and Ninik Suhartini in this insightful book. As they point out, kampungs are neither informal nor irregular forms of planning and design. An absence of formality does not mark kampungs. Kampungs bring vitality and vibrancy to the city. Kampungs have their own planning systems. Western and Eurocentric planning practices that dominate Indonesia's urban planning and policy are not applicable. Kampungs must be seen as communities that self-organize and implement incremental adaptation to survive and thrive.

Deden Rukmana
Professor and the Chairperson
Department of Community
and Regional Planning
Alabama Alabama A&M University
Huntsville, USA

References

Porter L (2011) Informality, the commons and the paradoxes for planning: concepts and debates for informality and planning. Plan Theory Prac 12(1):115–120

Roy A (2005) Urban informality: toward an epistemology of planning. J Am Plan Assoc 71(2):147–158

United Nations, Department of Economic and Social Affairs, Population Division (2019) World Population Prospects: The 2018 Revision (ST/ESA/SER.A/420). New York: United Nations

Yiftachel O (2009) Theoretical notes on 'gray cities': the coming of urban apartheid? Plan Theory 8(1):88–100

Preface

Urbanization continues as a major growth phenomenon in nearly all countries of the world, with many countries still struggling to find and apply appropriate tools of management. While urbanization in the neoliberal era provides many positive benefits in improving living standards, it has been shown that major structural changes to enhance access to decent housing, social development, equity, inclusion, basic infrastructure and service provision does not necessarily follow the former trend. In this setting, informal urbanization and myriad types of urban development emerging from informal governance arrangements, rising poverty, unequal access to resources, and the self-organized initiatives of residents, households, and communities have emerged to fill gaps in meeting day-to-day needs. This has become the norm in both the Global South and Global North, but primarily in the Global South where informality including informal housing production is the major contributor to housing supply.

The most visible expression of informality and informal urban development in the Global South is reflected in the upward growth trajectory of informal settlements and slums. These settlement types accommodate a growing class of urban disadvantaged and more recently an increasing middle class seeking affordable housing and basic services. These trends in city development increasingly ask questions of whose interests the city serves, the arrangements by which the city is built and produced, and who are the array of various stakeholders and their development agendas that mold these actions and processes that include some residents but not others.

In this setting, our interest in preparing this book has evolved out of our desire to deconstruct and further understand the making and shaping of informal settlements as occurring through the bottom-up initiatives of residents, households, and communities in their nuanced contexts. In the Global South, a significant portion of affordable housing delivery occurs through self-organization as driven by the initiatives of residents. This is an incremental approach to housing provision and upgrading whereby materials, financing, labor, social capital, and governance arrangements facilitate and underpin 'build as you go' activities by residents, households, and communities. City making by such stakeholders including the provision of adequate shelter, land tenure security, basic services, infrastructure, and livelihoods can be viewed as a desire by disadvantaged residents to achieve a reasonable and basic quality of life. While the latter 'self-build' in-situ approaches have received varied support in countries of the Global South, upgrading of housing is still dominated through a formal suite of 'top-down' housing policies and programs that still excludes many urban disadvantaged.

What receives comparatively little formal acknowledgment in the current debate on housing policies is that self-organized improvements by residents, households, and communities are in themselves a form of urban renewal worthy of support. Self-organized improvements to housing and community services outside the bounds of formal regulations and laws have become the main default mechanism of housing provision in many countries of the Global South, including Asia, and is now a reality reluctantly accepted by many governments. As self-organization activities and outcomes tend to be strongly nuanced and shaped by local contexts and drivers of change, they require additional time, resources, and sustained political commitment if the grassroot needs of residents and communities are to be understood and supported. A conundrum for governments in trying to find the best 'entry point' for support of upgrading is that at the human-scale level in informal settlements and slums, housing is incrementally improved through processes of self-organization, yet not in the manner the formal system desires and fully approves. The rigid codes and regulations of the formal system struggle to cope with the myriad housing adaptation practices expressed in informal settlements.

When experiencing everyday life in Indonesian cities and towns, it is not unusual to come into contact with someone who lives and resides in a kampung. This includes long-term generational residents, migrants, and newcomers such as university students seeking accommodation. Settlements known as kampungs are a key physical, social, and spatial unit of Indonesian society, with thousands of kampungs mow entrenched in the urban fabric. In Indonesian towns and cities, kampungs have been recognized as the equivalent to informal settlements and for some, slums. They have a long and changing history of attempts at upgrading and renewal, including efforts of the globally recognized and highly acclaimed Kampung Improvement Program (KIP). Kampungs increasingly accommodate the bulk of the urban disadvantaged and a growing lower middle class as the government and the private sector are unable to formally meet the rising demand for affordable housing.

Using the kampung phenomena, our desire for new knowledge is driven by the need to understand and analyze the nature of self-organization including processes shaping and making the kampung. In combination with other informal activities in public and private spaces, the varying array of kampungs anchored in local contexts collectively comprises the wider self-organized city. By exploring what self-organization in kampungs looks like, this will assist in deconstructing the processes, actions, and outcomes that create this unique brand of informality that is beyond simple mainstream conceptions of informality. When viewed from afar and at a larger scale, the latter are invariably couched in negative and adverse terms, thus devaluing the local circumstances of residents, households, and communities and their contribution to the wider city.

Through exploring the context of kampungs in Indonesia, our interest is in deepening an understanding of both (i) the activities, practices, and processes that emerge and create the notion of self-organization, and (ii) the outcomes of self-organization as expressed in kampungs. We posit that like other informal settlements and slums, kampungs and the processes of self-organization are integral to understanding the self-organized city. In other words, without understanding the role and nature of self-organization, one cannot understand the full workings of the contemporary global city, especially in the Global South. The self-organized city must be seen as an expression of the diverse range of social norms and values of residents, households, and community groups who are part of a larger complex system that self-organize and, in some cases, self-govern.

From the viewpoint of the evolution of the city, the concept of self-organization is fundamental to understanding how cities spontaneously evolve and adapt to changing circumstances using bottom-up activities and processes. By exploring self-organization, we understand more deeply who really plans and makes the city, especially processes shaping informality and expressions of informal urbanism such as informal settlements. From this perspective, the concept is beyond standard conceptualizations of informality, a universal yet traditional concept rooted in middle-class origins and which has become central to understanding and explaining city development, especially in the Global South. At its essence, we argue the formal–informal construct should be used as a starting point to explore and understand pivotal concepts central to city making, not an end point. This includes embracing not only self-organization, but related and overlapping concepts and processes of self-help housing, order, complex adaptive systems, emergence, and the use of material increments.

At a wider level, it is hoped that the knowledge and lessons shared in this book on self-organization and the processes underpinning how cities are really made can have an impact in two areas. Firstly, from the perspective of the author's being leading academics who teach undergraduate and postgraduate planning, design and architecture students, the book supports the overdue task of realigning and correcting the narrow western Euro-centric planning and design curriculum and pedagogy as taught in learning institutions. As a general observation, the latter doesn't address the nature of informality, emergence, ground-level urbanism, and the important role informal settlements play in city development. The foundational role of the informal city in city development is too often ignored. By dealing with the urban reality 'as it is' including what local contexts mean, rather than jumping too quickly to the question 'what solutions should be', aspiring students—the future leaders of tomorrow—can be exposed to the complexities, realities, and solutions for the contemporary global city. It is in the latter where informality and informal settlements and slums are commonplace challenges, thus requiring a major shift in planning and design education for future practitioners working in the Global South.

Secondly, greater knowledge and understanding of the role of self-organization can hopefully create more sympathetic responses by local and national governments to the housing needs of the urban disadvantaged based on in-situ approaches. This will require contextual approaches and a realignment in how policymakers see and view informal settlements, their residents and communities. The latter will contribute to collectively reaching the ambitious yet necessary global policies as contained in the New Urban Agenda and the Sustainable Development Goals (SDGs), particularly the SDG 11.1. The latter seeks to ensure access for all to adequate, safe, and affordable housing and basic services including upgrading of slums. Leveraging off and utilizing the concept of self-organization will add substantially to achieving these policies.

Bandung, Indonesia   Paul Jones
August 2022   Ninik Suhartini

Acknowledgments

This book is developed from our two-year research in urban kampungs in Jakarta, Bandung, and Yogyakarta, Indonesia, which contain the largest area of informal settlements in Indonesia. The research was carried out during the COVID-19 pandemic which created circumstances which have been challenging for us in terms of conducting field surveys, adjusting methods as well as preparing and editing the monograph. Informal settlements have been the center of the COVID-19 outbreaks in Indonesia which required us to rearrange research plans according to the dynamics on the ground.

It is fortunate that we completed the book with the full support from our valued colleagues at the School of Architecture, Planning and Policy Development, Institut Teknologi Bandung. Special mention should be made of Associate Professor Sri Maryati who has strongly supported and encouraged our research in kampungs since 2014; our research assistants Mahfira Azka Maharani, Muhammad Rizki Rayani Ramadhani, and Muhammad Sulton Asofyan; community representatives in Lebak Siliwangi and Tamansari Bandung, Kampung Marlina-Jakarta, and Kampung Purwokinanti Pakualaman-Yogyakarta. This research was funded by PPMU Research Grant of SAPPK ITB 2021 and P3MI Research Grant of SAPPK ITB 2020.

Our highest appreciation is also directed to Professor Deden Rukmana from the University of Alabama, who as a leader in the field of Indonesian urban planning studies willingly prepared the foreword of this book. Also, our thanks and gratitude to the independent reviewer who provided constructure comments and feedback on the draft book.

Our research will continue to expand key aspects of urbanization in the Global South so as to better understand myriad spectrums of formal, informal, and hybrid arrangements being developed and coevolved in building the city, as well as developing new research methodology to dissect, analyze and elaborate phenomena in informal settlements. This includes better understanding the processes that create self-help incremental housing.

Sydney, Australia   Paul Jones
Bandung, Indonesia   Ninik Suhartini

Contents

Abbreviations

BAPPENAS	National Planning Agency
GDP	Gross Domestic Product
KDP	Kecamatan Development Program
KIP	Kampung Improvement Program
KMB	Kelurahan Muara Baru
NGOs	Non-Government Organizations
NUSSP	Neighborhood Upgrading and Shelter Sector Project
PNPM	National Program for Community Empowerment
RPJMN	National Medium-Term Development Plan
RT	Rukun Tetangga or Neighborhood Unit
RW	Rukun Warga (RW) or Neighborhood Unit

Indonesian Vocabulary

bupati	A senior government official in charge of a county-level district known as a kabupaten
desa	Village communities and or groupings which have authority over the local people (including kampungs) in accordance with local traditions of the area
gang	Alleyway
gojek	Motorcycle taxi
hak guna bagunan	Rights and entitlements to build
hak milik	Freehold ownership of land
hak pakai	Land use rights
jalan	Street or road
kampung	Village including urban community being a settlement comprising a certain ethnic community, or mix thereof
Kelurahan	A urban subdistrict or community below the level of kecamatan government. A similar division to desa but with less autonomy
kota	'Fort', 'village,' 'town,' or a 'city' whose name is used to define the contextual characteristics of specific kampungs
kotaku	The National Slum Upgrading Program of Indonesia, part of the Cities Without Slums initiative
MCK	Abbreviation of *mandi, cuci, kakus* (communal sanitation facilities)
musrenbang	Development planning consultations
permukiman kumuh	A 'dirty settlement' used to describe a kampung as a slum
rencana kerja pemerintah	Government development plans
rencana kerja pemerintah daerah	Regional government development plans

Rukun Tetangga	Rukun Tetangga or Neighborhood Unit being the lowest administrative division. RTs comprise households
Rukun Warga	Rukun Warga or Neighborhood Unit being the second lowest administrative division. RWs comprise several RTs
rusunami	A type of leased vertical or high-rise housing which can be owned by the tenants at the end of the contract period
rusunawa	A type of rental vertical or high-rise housing
tribina	Physical, social, and economic development of a settlement
warung	A small family-owned business/store/stall

List of Figures

List of Tables

Chapter 1
Inquiring into Self-organization and the Self-organized City

Abstract As part of the process of urbanization, there has been an upward growth trajectory in the formation of informal settlements including slums. This is most pronounced in the Global South where a a significant portion of affordable housing, construction activities, services and infrastructure occur through self-organized activities. The latter is an incremental approach to housing provision and settlement upgrading whereby materials, financing, labor, social capital and governance arrangements combine to meet resident, household and community needs. Our exploration of the concept in both theory and practice is founded on the basic premise that the concept of self-organization is fundamental to understanding how cities spontaneously evolve and adapt to changing circumstances using bottom-up activities and processes. Self-organizing processes using residents, households and communities plus institutions results in unexpected outcomes. Through exploring three case study kampungs (informal settlements) in Indonesia, our interest is in deepening an understanding of: (i) the activities, practices and processes that emerge and create self-organization and (ii) the outcomes of self-organization as expressed in kampungs.

Keywords Self-organization · Global-South · Informality · Informal settlements · Slums · Kampung · Beyond informality

1.1 Introduction

When experiencing everyday life in Indonesian cities and towns, one is quickly exposed through our visual encounters to the complexity and outcomes of human behaviour. Our engagement with the city is first and foremost through the perception and processing of images, combining social, physical and spatial patterns as generated by residents who construct and navigate built and unbuilt spaces (Lynch 1964). To survive in the city, residents both consciously and unconsciously cross-over from formal to informal rules and protocols and vice versa to better meet their needs and that of their households. These practices, including how we engage, understand and adapt to such varying contexts and their nuanced meanings, is all part of everyday urbanism in Indonesian cities, and arguably the contemporary global city.

In the Global South including low and middle-income countries in Asia, Latin America, Africa and the Caribbean, there has been an ongoing debate that the process of urbanization is producing cities that are chaotic, disordered and dysfunctional. This has emerged due to the myriad types of urban development arising from informal governance arrangements, poverty and unequal access to resources, as well as neo-liberalism. Informal urban development in the Global South is most visibly expressed in the upward growth trajectory of informal settlements and slums. In the Asia Pacific region, for example, the UNESCAP 2015 report *The State of Asian and Pacific Cities 2015* highlighted that the region accommodated the world's biggest slums and informal settlements in addition to the largest concentrations of people living below the poverty line (UNESCAP 2015). Such trends increasingly elevate the housing crisis faced by the urban disadvantaged and poor, as well as question whose interests the city serves, the arrangements by which the city is produced, and the various stakeholders involved in such processes.

Kropf (2009) observed that the diversity and complexity of human settlements has elevated the need for various innovative means to describe, understand and conceptualize such phenomena. Cities are divided and joined by visible and invisible borders, where the physical divide is characterized by social, cultural and economic exclusion. Significant proportions of city residents are often excluded on attributes over which they have no control. This includes gender, age, religion, ethnicity, their perceived social status and importantly, the type, form and appearance of their housing, such as those expressed in informal settlements and slums. Residents of informal settlements and slums suffer greater spatial, social, and economic exclusion from the benefits and opportunities enjoyed by other stakeholders in the city. This rationale has been one driver of 'top down' and 'bottom up' upgrading schemes to improve living conditions and assist in providing a way out of poverty for the urban disadvantaged (Fig. 1.1).

Fig. 1.1 Informal settlements and slums such as these riverside settlements in Bangkok are a global challenge. *Source* Authors (2018)

In this setting, we can gain greater knowledge about cities by challenging and engaging with the multiple meanings of built form, use, notions of upgrading and appearance and, importantly, the people and the 'how and why' of their actions (Jones 2020). We also learn that formal planning regulations and policies often have little impact on many residents who make and sustain their lives in informal settlements through practices of self-organization. As a result, informality as seen in the self-organizing city is most visibly expressed in informal settlements—that is, spontaneous housing, informal architecture and associated spatial and physical patterns built from the 'bottom up' at the individual or group level. This is part of a complex system made of many parts—people, institutions, governance, orders, rules and materiality—which is constantly changing to accommodate and meet individual and collective needs.

So, why the interest in bottom-up self-organization and the self-organized city? Why should we be concerned with built form and spaces where residents and groups undertake self-help housing and social adaptations in neighborhoods that can be termed informal settlements? In the Global South, a significant portion of affordable housing, service and infrastructure delivery occurs through self-organized activities, which may be assisted or not. It is an incremental approach to housing provision and upgrading whereby materials, financing, labor, social capital and governance arrangements facilitate and underpin 'step by step' and 'build as you go' activities and processes. While the latter has received some support in countries of the Global South, these 'stop-start' efforts at upgrading are still seen as contravening official standards as the upgrading of housing remains outside of national and local government driven attempts as part of a formal suite of housing policies (Satterthwaite 2019). In this context, this book explores the nature of self-organized housing, and bottom-up urban renewal and upgrading that are individually and collectively characterized as being informal.

At its essence, the self-organized city is an expression of urban culture and social norms and values of residents and groups who are part of a larger complex system that self-organize and, in some cases, self-govern (Suhartini and Jones 2020). We define the self-organization model as one where plans are derived and developed within the system rather than being applied externally. In this context, an essential trait of self-organization is that it occurs without the help of a central authority, one result being that people, materiality and institutions of varying influence combine to create unexpected outcomes including informal architecture and irregular morphology. This combination introduces not only new and readjusted power relationships, but unex-pected dynamics. This reinforces the notion that the concept of self-organization is just as much about processes as it is outcomes. Understanding self-organization therefore is a key process which allows cities to dynamically recalibrate their socio-spatial patterns, form and structure based on their capacity to self-organize as new determinants evolve (Alfasi and Portugali 2007; Batty 2017).

When we interact and connect with the form, structure and sociality of towns and cities at myriad scales, we experience everyday urbanism. This includes the built form characteristics as expressed by its people and their practices to meet housing and related needs. These physical and social expressions inform us of how people live, their needs and the systems they use to go about their daily lives. It also includes small scale expressions of urban renewal and upgrading which may be undertaken informally by residents, households and communities, or be formally assisted by government, private sector and civil society. In this context, upgrading, which has been defined as measures undertaken by government and/or civil society to improve the quality of existing housing-built form and provision of housing and community-related infrastructure and services in settlements deemed informal settlements or slums, includes the important in-situ upgrading initiatives of residents and households (Satterthwaite 2019).

Increasing official disinterest in addressing the continued upward growth trajectory of informal settlements including slums poses major challenges to making progress on achieving the globally-accepted goal of inclusive urbanization as contained in the Sustainable Development Goals (SDGs). SDG 11, for example, which aims to create 'safe, resilient, inclusive and sustainable cities', will remain a distant aspiration unless we address the informal living and working conditions of the urban disadvantaged. While informal settlements and slums with their irregular and adverse physical form, structure, and questionable social strata and demographics may be perceived as problems by policy makers, it should be acknowledged that there has been a small, gradual shift to tolerate and implicitly accept these alternative forms of city making. This has occurred despite strong and sometimes repressive formal planning rhetoric, policies and upgrading schemes put in place by governments and other formal institutions.

City making as driven by disadvantaged residents and minority groups can be viewed as a desire by such residents to achieve a reasonable quality of life and 'normalcy'. This includes adequate shelter, land tenure security, the provision of basic services and infrastructure, and livelihoods. What receives little formal acknowledgement is that self-organized improvements by households and communities, such as those comprising kampungs, are in themselves a form of urban renewal (Kamalipour and Dovey 2020). At the micro-level, housing is incrementally improved and made livable via the provision of secure land tenure, social services, and basic infrastructure, yet not in the manner the formal system desires. As discussed in Chap. 2, contemporary research previously looked primarily at macro policy and tenure details of informal settlements (McCartney and Krishnamurthy 2018). As a result of examining such phenomena at a large scale, the important role of contextual nuances emerging via ground level urbanism was bypassed and generalisations were made which oversimplified and ignored person-land-community and settlement relationships at the human scale.

More recently, morphological inquiries at the micro-scale (settlement level, block patterns, housing and plot level) have investigated the informal codes guiding everyday life. This includes adaptation decisions such as building changes by informal settlement dwellers. The primary units of the urban fabric including 'buildings', 'plots', 'blocks' and 'streets' (see Marshall 2012, for example) are now being deconstructed to better understand socio-economic and spatial relationships and their outcomes. These recent studies are beginning to gain an understanding of the micro-level complexities of incremental additions undertaken through self-organization that are emerging as key elements of the upgrading and renewal processes (Jones 2021b). The different ways of producing urbanism from the 'bottom up' are most profound in informal settlements, with these processes as generating unexpected outcomes now being recognized as the rule, not an aberration or exception (Fig. 1.2).

There are number of reasons why these communities are now allowed to continue to engage in the process of (re)shaping cities. One key reason is that informal settlements facilitate flexible options to access housing sub-markets, a process which government themselves are unable to provide at the scale required. Informal settlements are increasingly being developed through a continuum of governance arrangements from top-down, bottom-up to hybrid. Thus, a multiplicity of governance arrangements is at play in creating and sustaining housing needs (Suhartini and Jones 2014). Despite this gradual shift in the way informal settlements are seen as being organized and managed, current conceptualisations of informality—specifically informal settlements and slums—do not capture the strong relationships between sectors, stakeholders, social and physical form that drives the formation of the self-organized city. The existing capacities and structures of urban governance and planning driven by formal structures and top-down mantras are generally insufficient to effectively engage and integrate with alternative and sometimes 'messy' forms of city making based on multiple expressions of adaptation. As a result, formal

Fig. 1.2 Incremental additions in informal settlements are a hallmark features of self-organized changes to housing, as seen in these vertical adaptations in Kampung Tamansari, Bandung. *Source* Authors (2018)

planning approaches incorporating simplistic land use plans, regulations and codes still dominate ways of resolving the 'informal settlement problem'.

1.2   Our Interest in Informality

Set within the context of Indonesia, the world's 4th largest population with 56.6% of the population urbanized (Statisca 2022), this book explores the phenomena of informal settlements through the lens of what self-organisation looks and feels like in kampungs. These unique settlements have been classed as informal settlements (Alzamil 2018; Rukmana 2018), having the highest levels and mixed forms of informality and illegality amongst all the differing settlement types comprising towns and cities in Indonesia. As discussed in Chap. 4, kampungs have a special place in the fabric of Indonesian settlements, originating out of a process of establishing a 'dual city' as put in place and regulated by colonial powers. The taxonomic diversity of kampungs means there are many different types of urban and rural kampungs which can be classified by land ownership (legal/illegal/hybrid), ethnic group and migrant mix, built condition (including those that fall into the category of slum), level of services and infrastructure, density and overcrowding. In urban areas, kampungs accommodate the majority of low-income households being characterized by incremental growth, self-financing and step-by-step construction, as well as shared basic services and infrastructure. Through processes of self-organization, urban kampungs have survived and expanded to accommodate longtime generational residents and new migrants to the city (World Bank 2016). Importantly, they provide affordable housing and the choice of multiple housing sub-markets for new migrants (see Fig. 1.3). In this setting, kampungs can be conceptualized by the diversity of their different types.

As towns and cities have expanded and incorporated kampungs within their spatial patterns, they now accommodate the bulk of the urban disadvantaged, including a growing middle class seeking affordable housing. The lack of affordable and accessible formal housing has driven the upward growth and densification of kampungs, including providing for diverse housing sub-markets. There are now tens of thousands of kampungs in Indonesia differentiated by location, demographic mix, ethnicity, socio-economic status, tenure security, housing quality, population density, governance arrangements, access to basic services and the environmental condition. For example, in Indonesia's second largest city, Surabaya, approximately 60% of the population resides in kampungs while in the national capital, Jakarta, there are over six hundred kampungs dispersed throughout the city (Coalition for Urban Transitions 2021).

At a Global level, there are various terms used to define informal settlements, given such terms reflect their specificities in differing contexts and settings. These range from Favelas (Brazil), Barriadas in Peru (Milone 1993), Villas Miserias (Argentina), Barriadas (Mexico), Poblaciones (Chile), Bidonvilles (Africa), Bustee in Bangladesh, Urban Village (Pacific Island Countries) to the Gecekondu in Turkey (Jones 2016a:

Fig. 1.3 Swathes of kampungs accommodating many types of housing sub-markets define the edges of the Tamansari Valley, Bandung. *Source* Authors (2019)

Neuwirth 2004). In Indonesia, it has been acknowledged in both theory and practice that self-organization via self-help housing and other initiatives are best represented by the kampung: an urban settlement characterized not only by informality, irregularity and illegality, but also by its resilience and flexibility of social and physical practices (Suhartini and Jones 2020; United National General Assembly 2013). Indonesia's formal housing policies and programs, such as those supporting public and self-help housing, have not been able to keep pace with the scale of the housing demand for the urban poor (Rukmana 2018). The kampung system makes a substantial contribution towards accommodating the housing and related needs of the urban disadvantaged and other housing sub-markets (Tunas and Peresthu 2010) (Fig. 1.4).

Our desire for new knowledge is driven by the need to understand the substance of self-organization shaping and making the kampung, thus pushing back layers that create this unique brand of informality that is beyond traditional large-scale analysis and mainstream conceptions of informality. Through exploring the context of kampungs in Indonesia, our interest is in deepening an understanding of (i) the activities, practices and processes that emerge and create self-organization and (ii) the unexpected outcomes of self-organization as expressed in kampungs. This interest is founded on the basic premise that the concept of self-organization is fundamental to understanding how cities spontaneously evolve and adapt to changing circumstances using bottom-up activities and processes. It provides new and different ways of looking and understanding informality. From this perspective, the concept is beyond basic conceptions of informality, a universal but necessary concept to understand, explain and improve city development, especially in the Global South.

Fig. 1.4 The native urban village of Hanuabada is an informal settlement in Port Moresby, Papua New Guinea. *Source* Paul Jones

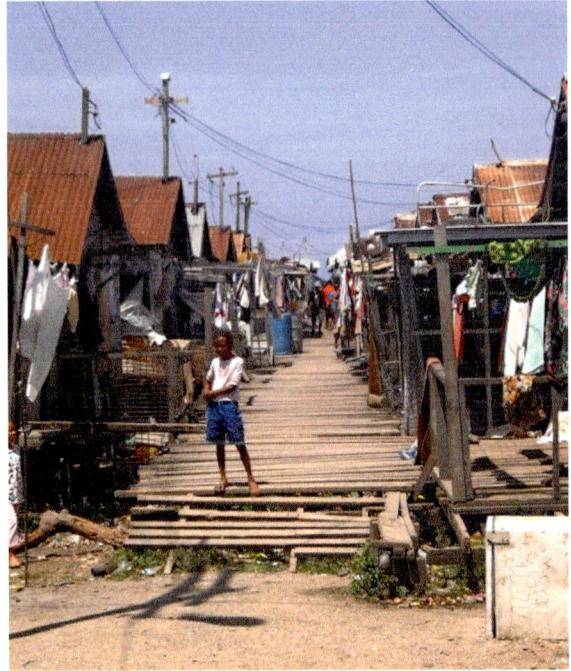

While terms such as the urban disadvantaged, urban poor and informal settlements are broad categorisations describing aspects of the 'urban divide', the Asian city is being increasingly made and shaped by informal practices and residents who are categorized as the 'have nots' and underprivileged (UNESCAP 2015). In the Indonesian context where local patterns of urbanization vary across many islands and cities, kampungs play a vital role in this process. Unless there is a full site redevelopment, housing in kampungs is renewed in a piecemeal fashion unlike other settlement types. Various factors come together to facilitate incremental building and land use practices, including when money is accumulated, if materials can be sourced and stored, the state of local governance to support or not support change, and when friends or community members can contribute their skills and time. In these circumstances, a wall may be erected, a verandah overhang enclosed, a roof added or improved, or another room constructed. While housing may be perceived as inadequate in kampungs, especially with respect to land tenure, building quality standards and infrastructure and services, they provide an important microcosm of innovative practices in adaptation and self-organization.

This book challenges the boundaries and usefulness of the often ambiguous formal-informal dichotomy of cities by recognizing informal settlements—in this case, kampungs—as dynamic places formed by self-organization and underpinned by rules, order and governance processes. While we apply the 'informal settlement' generalization to kampungs, we acknowledge that categorizing them under this broad term does not encapsulate the diversity of practices defining the formal-informal continuum that both shapes and makes urban kampungs and the wider city (Suhartini and Jones 2020). *Beyond the Informal: Understanding Self Organized Kampungs in Indonesia* argues that the current conception that a settlement is designated 'informal' carries little weight in gaining a deeper understanding of kampungs. The latter are in a sense strongly formed and regulated by their own contextualized and established protocols, behavioural rules and socio-cultural etiquette. That is, while classed as informal, they have their own nuanced form of formality being a complex subsystem that is part of the larger city complex system.

Our narrative is anchored on the premise that kampungs are neither informal nor irregular forms of planning and design as their behaviour accords with established rules and order which challenges traditional conceptions of informality (and formality); they are beyond standard interpretations of informal. Practices of self-organization give kampungs their own personalized means of shaping form, order and social practices. The commonplace usage of the term 'informal' when applied from a distance and at a larger scale does not engage in the details of 'human scale' urbanism. We argue that kampungs are not marked by an absence of mainstream notions of formality. Rather, a deeper and more holistic approach is needed where kampungs are recognized as opportunities for enriching the diversity, functionality and vitality of the city (Fig. 1.5).

As academic teachers and researchers strongly active in this field, we posit that normative planning and design education still has much catching up to do in terms of understanding and appreciating the resilience, rules and tenacity of residents who

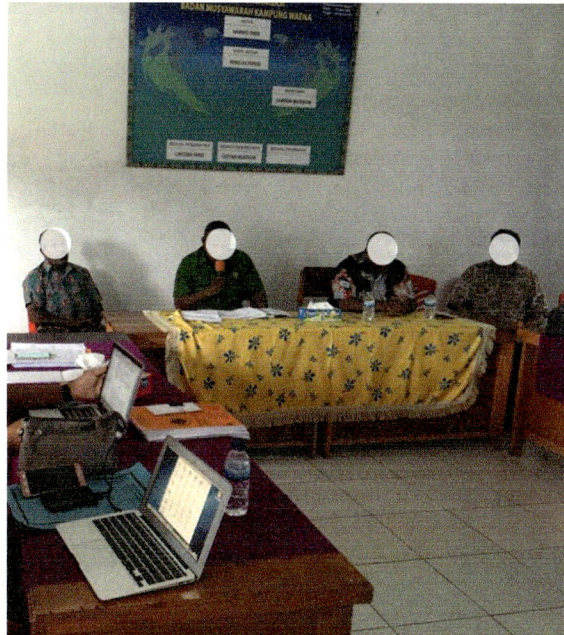

Fig. 1.5 Development Planning consultation in Kampung Waena, Papua, Indonesia. *Source* Ninik Suhartini (2020)

constitute the creation of self-organized informal settlements. Ways of looking at informal settlements and what they represent extend well beyond mainstream notions of informal. This book argues that kampungs have their own planning systems, rules and regulations. However, they are not the ones that students as future practitioners and leaders of tomorrow are being taught in their urban planning and design curriculum and pedagogy in places of higher education (Jones 2020).

It follows that a key tenet of this book is that the policy and rhetoric of informal settlements and slums as places of chaos, disorder and problems to be resolved through top-down planning and design remain as endemic simplistic narratives. They are developed from a position outside and beyond the contexts of understanding a deeper meaning of what constitutes informality. The negative implications associated with the term informality derive from a concept created by Western and Eurocentric planning and design policy—a practice that continues to permeate and be embedded in current planning and design education.

Kampungs, for example, are often not included in the development plans of Indonesian towns and cities, thus reflecting a reduced concern about the provision of basic infrastructure and services to vulnerable communities living and working in informal conditions. Western spatial planning practices dominate Indonesia's management of urbanization, where maps and colours, dots and line delineations are utilised to convey desired sets of implicit and explicit living standards that only middle- and higher-income groups can afford. These 'top-down' approaches demonstrate little understanding of the dynamics and socio-physical complexity of informal settlements and slums. Importantly, this includes rules and the sense of order of how residents and communities self-organize their built and unbuilt spaces through differing adaptation measures.

The dualistic concept is a basic approach used in the context of classifying development as illegal and legal, formal and informal. This formal-informal approach based on strong bipolarity is an obsolete conceptualization, having been the basis for many renewal and regularization programs where the main objective was to bring the 'disorder' of informality up to the standards and rules associated with 'planned order' (Jones 2017). As a concept created and developed by the formal planning system, the term informality is used by policymakers, planners and designers who usually do not live in or have experienced first-hand the people and communities comprising informal settlements and slums. By applying the 'formal-informal' binary, an intended or unintended consequence is to divide communities with negative connotations and the perpetuation of the 'haves and have nots'.

The concept, with its adverse stigma, is created and applied by people beyond the realms of having a deeper understanding of informality. It is not used constructively by government institutions to examine the uneasy power relationships between city stakeholders. This includes residents, the private sector, as well as the city and national governments that are so pronounced in the making of cities of the Global South and developing world. The emergence and growth of informality does not unpack the role of power relations. It is important to understand how power is applied and used between various city stakeholders in redefining the fluid boundaries between what is acceptable practice and not acceptable, the legal and so-called illegal. The valuable contribution of those making their lives in informal settlements to the wider processes of homemaking, city building and belonging in the contemporary city receives little traction in development processes (Dovey et al. 2017).

If we move beyond the simplistic dichotomy of formal and informal construct, the city emerges as comprising numerous complex subsystems representing multiple configurations emerging from a formal-informal continuum. These subsystems organize, secure and manage the distribution of resources and power, albeit unequally across time and space. Depending on the prevailing social-cultural systems and administration of governance and power arrangements, there will be many permeations in the outcomes achieved. At the same time, there will be countless parallel processes of negotiation on various levels regarding the use and access to power and resources.

From this perspective, the city is a site of contestation and mobilization being created by a wide range of stakeholders who have many self-interests, practices and processes in achieving their development objectives. Some stakeholders wield and have access to power far greater than others such as local government councillors, developers, planners and designers. Others like civil groups and community leaders may not be well known, but still hold significant influence over decision-making processes at the local level. The city is a dynamic playground for the negotiation of power and resources within and across systems, with much local expression of urbanism occurring in informal settlements. At a broader level, informality and planned settlements can be seen as a product of capitalism's uneven mode of development, accelerated by neo-liberalization and trends in globalization. The changing city fabric is thus a continuum of formal and informal activities and outcomes, representing the collation of all forms and types of regulated, partly-regulated and deregulated systems of the urban milieu. It is not the simple formal-informal binary (Suhartini and Jones 2019) (Fig. 1.6).

Through the examination of kampungs strongly shaped by local contexts in different Indonesian cities, our work aims to extend ways of thinking about informal settlements and their socio-physical adaptation strategies. We seek to reinforce the need to understand different contexts and the 'city as it is' rather than the modernist preoccupation with formal solutions of 'how it should be'. This includes understanding current approaches which aim to 'formalize' informal settlements to 'cleanse' and correct kampungs of their problems, thus realigning residents to new and different social and physical norms and values (Jones 2017). We strongly argue that kampungs should not be judged according to their often-adverse physical appearance and form—that is, the initial visual image formed from our physical and material encounters with the city. Rather, they should be assessed according to the value that kampungs hold to its users through their practices of self-organization and wider contribution to city making.

This book highlights how informal settlements are not places of unplanned physical configurations that are often judged, conceptualised and critiqued from *Beyond Informality* through formal lenses. First and foremost, they are communities that self-organize and implement adaptation and incremental strategies to survive. The focus of this book therefore is on the 'how and why' of self-organization and incremental

Fig. 1.6 The city is a site of
contestation at many scales,
as seen through the
negotiated placement of
these two intersecting
balconies in Kampung Lebak
Siliwangi. *Source* Authors
(2018)

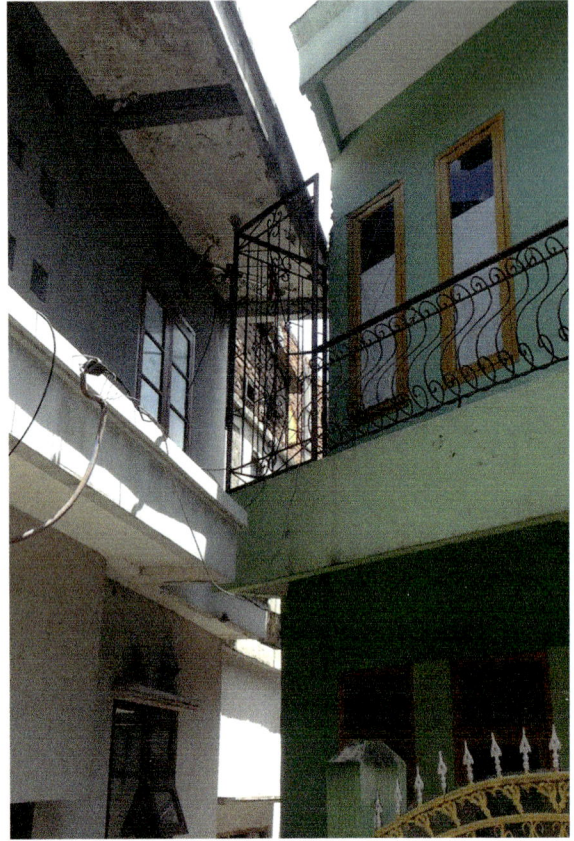

adaptation. We seek to show that many kampungs are beyond mainstream conceptualizations of Informality by having their own rules, order and set of actors which
shape their decision-making and social and physical complexity. Kampungs mould
the type of self-organization that emerges and crafts the kampung while remaining
embedded within its unique spatial context. Kampungs self-regulate and adapt via
changing rules, socio-economic circumstances and balancing different interests. As
we have argued elsewhere (Suhartini and Jones 2019, 2020), kampungs have their
own governance processes representing one of many subsystems which connects with
other systems to determine how resources and services are allocated and distributed.

By viewing the kampung as a key element in the Indonesian city fabric, the
meaning and complexity of the self-organized city in the Indonesian context is better
understood. While the negative definitions as applied by formal institutions, policymakers and some academics have strongly influenced policies and plans towards
informal settlements, kampungs are inseparable entities of urban form and structure that contribute significantly to the development of contemporary cities in

Indonesia. Their organization represents alternative forms of hybrid urban governance which have already been shown to work successfully in parts of Indonesia. Despite constraints on resources and other potential beneficial systems of decision-making, including access to services and basic standards of housing, kampung governance processes aspire in their own unique way to provide the best levels of security, socio-cultural and religious wellbeing, sociality and economic prosperity. There is an ongoing process where governance processes seek a balance in terms of access to power and resources as well as recognition of their legitimacy and 'legality' in the eyes of wider urban stakeholders (Suhartini and Jones 2019) (Fig. 1.7).

It is this perspective of valuing kampung urbanism and governance that needs to be considered by urban planners and policymakers so as to understand the holistic processes of urbanization in cities of developing countries. This is important for policymakers if there is to be a sincere desire in working towards better urban outcomes for all city residents, as proclaimed by countries in Habitat III: 'leave no one behind' and the urban SDG 11. This book highlights how kampungs are *Beyond Informality* and are not chaotic physical configurations with disjointed governance and social structures. By analysing everyday practices by which institutions and people construct and govern society, we gain a deeper understanding of the processes of 'becoming' and emergent urbanism (Dovey et al. 2017).

Fig. 1.7 Despite their often adverse environmental and physical condition, kampungs are a key element of Indonesian life. *Source* Authors

In kampungs, self-organized strategies are used as a major supplier of housing production and small-scale commercial activity. Quality of life in informal settlements including livelihoods, household stability, coherent governance, sociality and participation in communal and religious events is dependent on how households, residents and their governance arrangements self-organize via rules and governance and implement their incremental adaptive strategies. In this book, our interest in self-organization in kampungs seeks to investigate the following:

1. What is the concept of self-organization and other key notions which shape the contemporary city?
2. By using case studies, how do we see the process of self-organization as expressed in kampungs?
3. What are the implications of the kampung model of self-organization and the implications for urban planning and design?

With informal urbanization being the dominant mode of city making in the twentieth first century, this book provides a much-needed analysis of self-organization and adaptation strategies of the urban kampung in Indonesia's urbanization process. In the context of planning and design education, this book provides a better understanding on how one needs to consider human-scale urbanism so as to achieve more effective and efficient plans and policies in the self-organized city. Although self-organization by residents comes with its challenges as outlined in the book, formal planning in both Indonesia and other developing countries have much to learn from understanding self-organized settlements (kampungs) and informal settlements 'as they are'.

This work on informal settlements in Indonesia is important for several reasons. Firstly, it acknowledges the self-organized bottom-up processes by which affordable housing is produced, especially in cities of the Global South including Southeast Asia. By understanding self-organization practices, this work provides strong arguments to review the dynamics of self-help housing efforts and how they can be supported in practice. Secondly, this work unpacks processes and outcomes of incremental adaptation so as to understand at a deeper level how the physical form of housing evolves and is configured and reconfigured. Most importantly, we see the steps of adaptation and self-organisation as expressions of the relationship between social and physical complexity and vice versa, appreciating and acknowledging forms of vernacular and local urbanism. Thirdly, by analysing the processes and outcomes of self-organized incremental adaptations, we learn about the rules, governance and orders by which change occurs. These are all essential in changing ways of seeing, designing and planning inclusive cities.

This book concludes by discussing implications for practice if informal settlements and their communities can move *Beyond Informality* and have their key social and economic role in the self-organizing city recognized and valued. This includes confronting the adverse impacts of unregulated adaptive incremental design by residents and households on the environmental condition of informal settlements. Many informal settlements have already 'tipped over' in terms of overcrowding, poor sanitation, air quality, drainage and ventilation. In relation to planning and design practice, this book provides a better understanding in how one needs to consider human-scale urbanism to achieve more effective and efficient planning plans and policies.

Finally, the research contained in this book comes from multiple sources. Using a case study approach (Yin 2014), three case studies were selected from Indonesia's most populous island, Java, and from Indonesia's three largest cities: Jakarta, Surabaya and Bandung. While the case study kampungs can be classed as informal settlements with mixed land ownership, density, morphology and varying historical drivers of development within an urban setting, they are not slums. Differentiating the varying types of kampungs that comprise and are synonymous with the centrality of the 'Indonesian informal city' is important and central to understanding the nature of contemporary Indonesian urbanism.

The persistent spread of the COVID-19 pandemic in 2020 and 2021 meant it was not possible, nor was it responsible for the health of ourselves plus research assistants to go outside of these jurisdictions. The interviews with residents and governance leaders in the three case studies occurred from February to May in 2021 while interviews with planning officials in the three respective Planning Boards, local planners, and academics from the Bandung Institute of Technology (ITB) occurred in the latter half of 2020. Information gained from interviews with residents of Lebak Siliwangi and Tamansari gained during an earlier field trip in April to June 2020 was also used.

The interviews have been supplemented with secondary materials from national and municipal planning documents, published and unpublished reports (all cited), and news magazine articles. The core narratives contained in this book have been developed from the theme of 'Better Understanding Informal Urbanism' which has underpinned an internationally acclaimed annual ITB Global Studio anchored in kampungs. The latter has been running under the auspices of the School of Architecture, Planning and Policy Development at ITB since 2014 and under the leadership of the two authors.

References

Alfasi N, Portugali J (2007) Planning rules for a self-planned city. Plan Theory 6(2):164–182. https://doi.org/10.1177/1473095207077587

Alzamil A (2018) Evaluating urban status of informal settlements in Indonesia: a comparative analysis of three case studies in north Jakarta. J Sustain Dev 11(4):148–173

Batty M (2017) The new science of cities. The MIT Press

Coalition for Urban Transition (2021) Siezing Indonesia's urban opportunity. Accessed from: https://coalitionforurbantransitions.org/en/publication/seizing-the-urban-opportunity/seizing-indonesias-urban-opportunity/

Dovey K, Pafka E, Ristic M (2017) Mapping urbanities: morphologies, flows, possibilities. Routledge, New York

Jones P (2016a) The emergence of Pacific urban villages—urbanization trends in the Pacific Islands. Pacific Studies Series, Asian Development Bank (ADB), Manila. Accessed from: https://www.adb.org/publications/emergence-pacific-urban-villages

Jones P (2017) Formalizing the informal: understanding the position of informal settlements and slums in sustainable urbanization policies and strategies in Bandung, Indonesia. J Sustain 9(8):1436. Accessed from: https://doi.org/10.3390/su9081436

Jones P (2020) The case for inclusion of international planning studios in contemporary urban planning pedagogy. J Sustain 11(15). Accessed from: http://dx.doi.org/10.3390/su11154174

Jones P (2021b) Distance and proximity matters: understanding housing transformation through micro-morphology in informal settlements. Int J Hous Pract Spec Ed Informal Hous Pract 21(2):1–27. Accessed from: https://doi.org/10.1080/19491247.2020.1818052

Kamalipour H, Dovey K (2020) Incremental production of urban space: a typology of informal design. Habitat Int 98:1–8. Accessed from: https://doi.org/10.1016/j.habitatint.2020.102133

Kropf L (2009) Aspects of urban form. Urban Morphol 105–120. Accessed from: file:///C:/Users/prjon/Downloads/UM_2009-02_105-20_Aspectsofurbanform.pdf

Lynch K (1964) The image of the city. MIT Press Academic

Marshall S (2012) Planning, design and the complexity of cities, in complexity theories of cities have come of age. In: Portugali J, Meyer H, Stolk E, Tan E (eds) Springer, Berlin. Accessed from: https://doi.org/10.1007/978-3-642-24544-2_11

McCartney S, Krishnamurthy S (2018) Neglected? Strengthening the morphological study of informal settlements. SAGE Open Monogr 8(1). Accessed from: https://doi.org/10.1177/2158244018760375

Milone P (1993) Kampung improvement in the small and medium sized cities of central java. Rev Urban Reg Dev Stud 5(1):74–94

Neuwirth R (2004) Shadow cities: a billion squatters, a new urban world. Routledge

Rukmana D (2018) Upgrading housing settlement for the urban poor in Indonesia: an analysis of the Kampung Deret program. In: Grant B, Yang Liu C, Ye L (eds) Metropolitan Governance in Asia and the pacific rim: borders, challenges, futures. Springer Nature Singapore. Accessed from: https://doi.org/10.1007/978-981-13-0206-0_5

Satterthwaite D (2019) Rethinking housing policies: Harnessing local innovation to address the global housing crisis. UCLG World Congress, Durban, South Africa. Accessed from: Rethinking_Housing_Policies_Harnessing_l.pdf

Statista (2022) Indonesia: urbanization from 2010 to 2020. Accessed from: https://www.statista.com/statistics/455835/urbanization-in-indonesia/

Suhartini N, Jones P (2014) Reframing approaches to conceptualising urban governance in Melanesia: insights from Jayapura and Port Moresby. J Reg City Plan 25(2):96–114

Suhartini N, Jones P (2019) Urban governance and informal settlements: lessons from the city of Jayapura, Indonesia. The Urban Book Series, Springer Nature, Switzerland

Suhartini S, Jones P (2020) Better understanding self-organizing cities: a typology of order and rules in informal settlements. J Reg City Plan 31(3):237–263. Accessed from: https://doi.org/10.5614/jpwk.2020.31.3.2

Tunas D, Peresthu A (2010) The self-help housing in Indonesia: the only option for the poor? Habitat Int 34(3):315–322

UNESCAP (2015) The state of Asian and Pacific cities 2015: Urban transformations shifting from quantity to quality. https://www.unescap.org/sites/default/files/The%20State%20of%20Asian%20and%20Pacific%20Cities%202015.pdf

United National General Assembly (2013) Report of the special rapporteur on adequate housing as a component of the right to an adequate standard of living, and on the right to non-discrimination in this context on her mission to Indonesia. Agenda Item 3, Human Rights Council, New York. Accessed from: file:///C:/Users/prjon/Documents/HOME%202020%20and%202021/Book%20and%20Slum%20Upgrading/To%20Read/52e0f5e7a%20RApportor.pdf

World Bank (2016) Indonesia urban story. Accessed from: https://www.worldbank.org/en/news/feature/2016/06/14/indonesia-urban-story

Yin R (2014) Case study research: design and methods (5th ed). SAGE Publications

Chapter 2
Informality and Responding to the Challenges of Informal Settlements

Abstract In cities of the Global South and the developing world, informal urbanization is now the primary mode of city making. A key feature of this trend is the rising growth of informal settlements and slums catering for the housing, and social and economic needs of city residents, households and their communities. Their expansion is increasingly driven by unprecedented migration, civil unrest and war, rising poverty, outdated planning policies and lack of access to affordable housing. Importantly, informal settlements and slums have become the main means of housing production for the urban disadvantaged and lower middle class in towns and cities of the Global South. Central to the process of making and transforming informal settlements is the major role of self-organized and self-help initiatives in building shelter in an incremental manner. The important role of self-organization has emerged through recognition that the process of housing transformation by residents, households and communities is typically incremental via small-scale socio-physical alterations and adaptations outside the realms of formal rules and regulations. Attempts at top-down upgrading informal settlements and slums have varied, with many focusing on 'formalizing the informal'.

Keywords Informality · Informal settlement · Indonesia · Self-organization · John Turner · Self-help

2.1 Introduction

The transition of the world's population from rural to urban as contained in towns and cities has occurred rapidly in the twentieth and twenty-first centuries. This urban phenomenon has led to the term 'planet of cities', an observation stressing the rise of often unmanaged urbanization (Angel 2012). Since the mid twentieth century, the proportion of people living globally in urban areas has risen from 30% (approximately 750 million people) in 1950, to 55% (approximately 4.2 billion people) in 2018. This figure is expected to reach approximately 68% by 2050 (UN-DESA 2018). Importantly, in Global South countries it is estimated that approximately 30% of urban dwellers live their lives in informal settlements including slums (UN-Habitat 2016).

In Asia, poverty remains one of the main reasons for the emergence of informal settlements, with the region containing 60% of the world's 1.25 billion poor (World Bank 2014). Millions of disadvantaged households are unable to afford housing due to limited housing supply, finances and a lack of affordable land (UN-Habitat 2015). Poor households spend a large part of their income on housing in combination with expenditure on other basic needs such as food, education and healthcare. One result of this situation is that poorer residents gravitate to informal settlements and slums as they provide affordable options in choosing housing sub-markets (UN-Habitat 2015). In 2015 in the Asia Pacific region, it was estimated that the region contained the world's biggest slums and informal settlements and the largest concentrations of people living below the poverty line (UNESCAP 2015). These trends raise questions regarding whose interests are being served by the city and the wider urbanization process, who are the stakeholders involved, and the arrangements by which informal settlements and their households self-organize and survive. More importantly, they highlight that the challenges facing growing numbers of the urban disadvantaged is a multi-faceted and cross-sector development task (Fig. 2.1).

Current projections show that disadvantaged people and those seeking better lifestyles will continue moving from rural to urban areas. By 2050, it is estimated that more than 3 billion people will live in informal settlements (UN-DESA 2018). This means most of the the world's population will be living in informal settlements

Fig. 2.1 Informal settlements and slums as built incrementally are commonplace in all towns and cities in the Asia–Pacific Region. *Source* Authors (2019)

within less than three decades. Much of the recent urbanization growth in developing countries has taken place in unplanned and informal settlements where basic services are few and tenure is insecure. As such, city making is being increasingly driven by disadvantaged residents and minority groups who self-organize, adapt and are innovative in their desire to achieve a reasonable quality of life. This includes adequate shelter, sociality and livelihoods (UN Habitat 2016).

In cities of the Global South and the developing world, informal urbanization—that is, urbanism produced outside the realm of legal regulations and official rules—is now the dominant mode of city making in the twenty-first century. Cities of the Global South and the developing world reflect myriad types of formal and informal urban development emerging from transformation, upgrading and renewal practices. The latter forms of urban development are most visibly expressed in the upward growth trajectory of informal settlements and slums, often driven by poverty, unequal access to resources and informal governance arrangements. For examples, in countries comprising Latin America and the Caribbean, it has been estimated some 30% to 60% of the housing stock is produced informally and is deemed sub-standard. Estimates of informal housing production as seen in informal settlements and slums in Asia and Africa is likely to be comparable or higher (Satterthwaite 2019). Processes of informal urbanization have become the norm rather than the exception. The result is that informal settlements are common in every city in Asia, Africa, and Latin America, and are becoming increasingly visible in developed Global North countries such as the United States, Canada and Australia (Harris 2018).

2.2 Informality and the Informal Settlement Context

The phenomenon of informality expressed in all aspects of life is most visible in rising rural–urban migration, unplanned development and transient populations (Avni and Yiftachel 2014). In the Global South where the symptoms of informality are most prominent, the term informality has a solid research base that has been undergoing major refinements since its introduction into the development discourse during the 1970s. The emergence of informality was most noticeable in the development of micro-scale commercial and informal economies in towns and cities of the Global South, especially in Africa and South America. Their expansion was increasingly driven by unprecedented migration, strong demographic growth and outdated planning policies. The spread of informality is now diverse, with informality estimated as the daily way of life for approximately a sixth of the world's population (Lehmann 2021).

The importance of informality and an 'informal sector' is associated with Hart's (1973) distinction between formal and informal economic sectors as based on types of employment observed in Africa. In the 1970s, the International Labor Office adopted the informal sector concept to describe small-scale activities that fell outside of formal recognition, enumeration and governmental regulations (International Labor Office 1972). These activities were categorized under the umbrella term 'informal economy'

Fig. 2.2 The informal economy is strongly associated with street markets and traders using well-connected public spaces at varying times of the day in Kampung Tamansari, Bandung. *Source* Authors (2020)

(Moser 1994). With increasing informal urbanization in Africa, Hart's work on the informal economy and informal sector saw the term 'informal' subsumed into usage in mainstream planning literature (Jones 2016b). Large and both visible and obscured tracts of informal housing became intimately connected with the growth of the informal economy, underemployment, poverty, a lack of access to basic services, social deprivation and tenure insecurity. The latter is a defining point between developed and developing countries given that informal settlements in developed countries often exist within the context of some form of formal land tenure rights and support from formal government (Fig. 2.2).

The rise of modernist planning, design and architecture at the beginning of the twentieth century saw the term informality used to define the dichotomy between formal and informal. The term formal was used conceptually and in a physical context to emphasize modernist aspirations of social and physical order (including ways of doing design and architecture), moral standards, health, and urban quality. It's usage replaced what was viewed as being abhorrent to the process and outcomes of city planning. Informality was purported to be the antithesis of modern planning and design, thereby relegating bottom-up and often spontaneously-driven actions that met the needs of the urban disadvantaged as being 'inferior' and 'second class'. With the rise of unregulated housing and illegal land development in the 1970s, the term informality morphed from its association with the activities of the informal economy, such as hawking and street stall sellers, into wider mainstream usage. This is reflected in terms like 'informal urbanism' and 'informal settlements', the latter incorporating informal housing. While informality retained its middle-class bias and roots, it was increasingly seen as an output of the processes of socio-economic exclusion, leading over time to the relaxation and lack of enforcement of rules governing pre-established orders.

As Franco notes (2021), informal activities are those that are unregulated by formal institutions, notwithstanding there are parallel social and legal environments which ensure the conformity of similar activities to the same rules which are only enforced in the formal sector. Avni and Yiftachel (2014) take an all-encompassing perspective and define urban informality as *"developments, populations and transactions which do not comply with planning or legal regulations, and are denied planning approval or full membership in the urban community"* (Avni and Yiftachel 2014: 487). In this setting, housing deemed as informal can be defined as being constructed without the formal approval of the authorities, including secure land title and tenure. Housing classed as informal does not meet specified legal standards for building, construction and planning (for example, the use of a specified type of building materials, connection to certain services, and setbacks from adjoining side and front boundaries). Questions also linger as to whether the housing is constructed on land that is legally owned and certified through State institutions by the inhabitants (Suhartini and Jones 2019).

As a result, the varying local incarnations of the term informal in the urban context including spontaneous, organic, vernacular, illegal, unauthorized and unplanned are used as 'catch all' phrases to encompass land use, development and communities that do not align with the rules, regulations and preconceptions that govern urban formal systems. These are terms that strongly reflect the type of formation and the emergence of place, activities and space that have been deemed informal. Not surprisingly, there is a prejudice against informality as reflected in law violations for land tenure and ownership, quality of built structures, physical appearance and spatial layout.

Within this context, the term informal settlements have become mainstream in deconstructing and understanding the condition of the contemporary city primarily in the Global South. While the appropriateness of the language, terminology and definitions surrounding 'informality' remain debatable, informal settlements have been identified as containing the poorest quality of housing, a lack of access to basic services, questionable legal land tenure and an absence of proper urban planning. In his work on urbanization and kampungs in Indonesia, Obermayr (2017) states that informal settlements are areas occupied by urban dwellers informally, with the land deemed not suitable for housing. Zarate (2016) defines informal settlements as those communities "not in compliance with building norms and property and urban planning regulations…" with such illegality leading to residents being displaced and criminalized (Zarate 2016: 1). Similarly, UN-Habitat (2015) defines informal settlements in more detail as *"residential areas where (1) inhabitants have no security of tenure vis-à-vis the land or dwellings they inhabit, with modalities ranging from squatting to informal rental housing, (2) the neighborhoods usually lack, or are cut off from, basic services and city infrastructure and (3) the housing may not comply with current planning and building regulations, and is often situated in geographically and environmentally hazardous areas"* (UN-Habitat 2015: 1). Residents invariably have to trade-off their amenity, housing and land tenure risks so they can reside in localities where they need to be for employment, be close to extended families, or can only access the housing sub-market they desire in that location only.

In an Indonesian context, defining features of informal settlements such as kampungs include their non-geometric and non-linear physical patterns, unclear

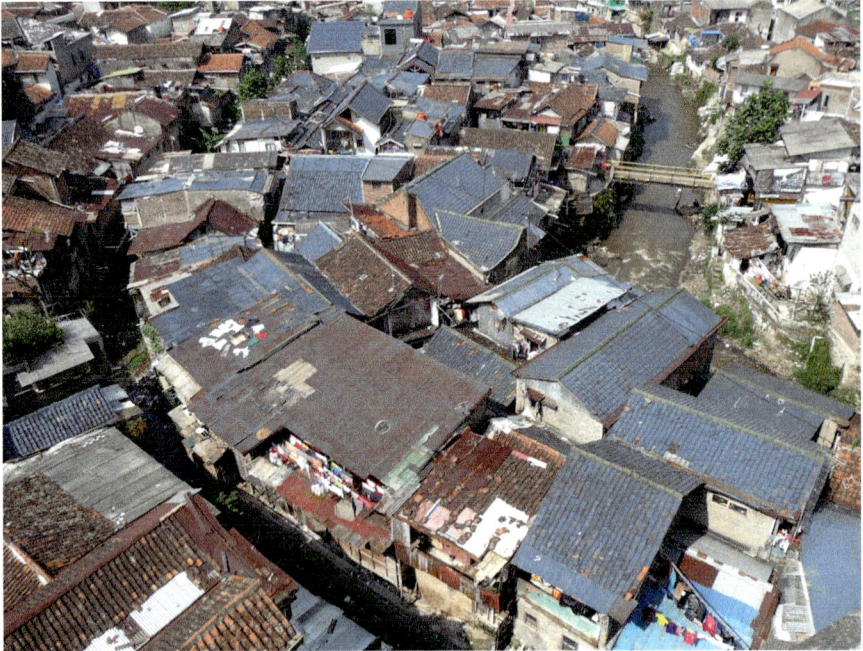

Fig. 2.3 The informal settlement (kampung) of Pulosari, Bandung, Indonesia, meets the criteria of an informal settlement including having high population density and being overcrowding. *Source* Authors (2018)

legal status of land, their often 'lower' socio-economic status and processes of establishment (Suhartini and Jones 2019). Rukmana (2018) observes that in informal settlements in Indonesian cities, housing is often illegally constructed on small plots using low-quality building and ad hoc recycled materials. These settlements have limited formal water supplies, poor drainage, narrow alleyways and footpaths, and minimal resources for solid waste management. Unsurprisingly, residents of informal settlements are both stigmatized and marginalized from afar (Fig. 2.3).

2.3 Attempts to Formalize Informal Settlements

With a major rise in urbanization globally in the 1960s and 70s and the accompanied growth in the informal sector, informal settlements and social movements promoting 'grassroots' housing, government policy regarding these concerns has slowly shifted. The modernist school of thought initially viewed informal settlements and slums as a necessary transitional structural phenomenon that facilitated economic activity as part of the process of urbanization. However, such theories now have little traction as a broad range of contemporary theories based on the global experience of urbanization and its positive and negative consequences highlight systemic failures of land and housing markets arising from demographic, economic and institutional factors (Fox 2013). Institutional issues, including illegal buildings and unclear land tenure which violates planning and building regulations and land laws, have all added to limiting the amount of public investment in social housing for the urban disadvantaged (UNESCAP 2015).

As a result, the persistence of informal settlements and slums have meant that many governments at a global level have been forced to confront the fact that informal settlements and slums exist because of or in response to the paucity of relevant public policies across a range of sectors. In many jurisdictions, governmental attitudes have shifted from one of initial hostility towards seeing low-income and urban disadvantaged groups as authentic builders and designers in myriad localities in the city, to providers of affordable and low-income housing. Over the last fifty years, the physical approaches employed by the government and private sectors have changed from the demolition of informal housing, the eviction of residents, and resettlement into low-income housing to the recognition of self-built housing through in-situ assistance and upgrading. The latter occurred initially in South America through the development of sites and services, tenure legalization, joint private and public housing schemes, plus the major support of international development partners. It has become clear that governments have accepted that they do not have the resources and capacity to meet the increasing demand for affordable housing, and that informal settlements play an important de-facto role that governments cannot fill (Fig. 2.4).

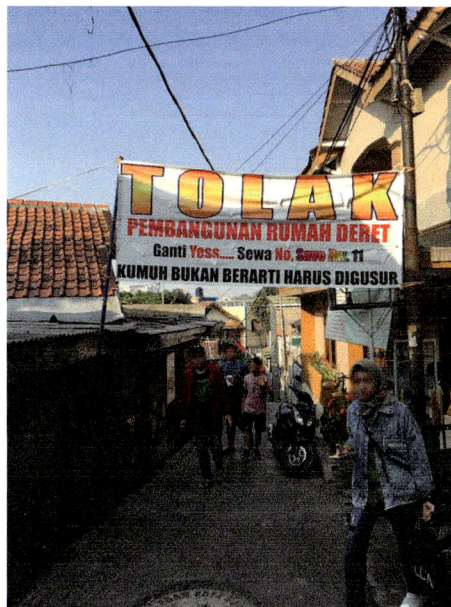

Fig. 2.4 Expression of community's resistance against attempts at the 'formalization of informal settlements' in Bandung. *Source* Authors (2019)

Leveraging self-help and self-organized initiatives in building shelter in an incremental and staged manner (for example, Turner 1976), many informal settlements in developing countries were subject to planned sites and services schemes. These were supported financially and promoted by international development agencies working with governments and residents. The sites and services schemes emerging in the 1970s reflected a process by which poor quality housing and the land on which they were sited were transformed into permanent housing on plots of an acceptable size with basic services. This support for informal settlements containing low-income housing combined basic services, provision of land, housing renewal and self-management under an overall framework of formal planning rules and conditions at the plot, block and neighborhood scale. Importantly, the economic principles of affordability, cost recovery and project replication were key aspects of sites and services projects applied in developing countries in the late twentieth century.

In the late 1980s and 1990s, the focus of formal support for informal and squatter settlements shifted in three main areas. Firstly, at a conceptual level, sites and services projects were considered too limited to address the complexities of the urban sector. As such, there was a shift from urban shelter at the level of the neighborhood to the urban sector. Development agencies like UN-Habitat and the World Bank substituted terms such as 'sites and services' with 'urban management programmes' (UMP), an approach applied strongly in Indonesia in the 1980s and 1990s. The approach moved from individual projects to a sector-wide perspective, addressing policy, institutional, regulatory, land tenure, health, education, economic development and financing aspects of upgrading at the city level. State-aided self-help projects were integrated into enabling urban policies at larger scales (Huchzermeyer and Misselwitz 2016). One result of this shift was that projects became complex with the addition of multiple sector-wide components, with project advancement dependent on the successful resolution of other sector and project parts. Thus, project implementation can become difficult, problematic and messy (Fig. 2.5).

Secondly, as part of the urban sector approach which considered the economic development implications of upgrading housing, the provision of housing in informal settlements now incorporated approaches centered on self-help solutions backed by institutional and regulatory reform. The successful application of the economic principles of affordability, cost recovery and project replication were argued by development agencies and banks as leading to greater financial control by the government, despite increased spending on land acquisition and infrastructure. However, this did not eventuate in practice as many of the project principles that were applied could not be maintained by the low-income target groups as they were unable to meet the user-paid service requirements. Many implementing government agencies also lacked the capacity and willingness to enforce project conditions at the local level (Sengupta and Shaw 2019).

Thirdly, the issuing of formal land title to residents was based on the principle that access to secure tenure was a trigger to access other development opportunities including credit and finance, public services and livelihood activities. Land tenure security was also a key component in justifying public expenditure in areas which, in most cases, needed retrofitting. Application of this principle was acknowledged

Fig. 2.5 Resident led self-organized and self-help housing in informal settlements and slums are major contributors to meeting the demand for shelter and housing affordability, as seen in the diverse expressions of roofing materials and styles in kampung Lebak Siliwangi, Bandung. *Source* Authors (2018)

as a key mechanism to break the vicious cycle of poverty. The innovative work on land tenure in informal settlements in Peru by De Soto (1989) was influential in encouraging international agencies to engage in large-scale formalization programs, including the provision of formal land tenure. The World Bank in 1993, for example, promoted security of land and housing tenure as the first priority in the housing sector, claiming its absence led to under-investment in housing and reduced housing quality and adequate shelter for all (World Bank 1993). If projects could not meet achievement of this project pre-condition in the field, future project funding was often withdrawn.

Despite the work by researchers such as De Soto (1989) which posited that formal approaches were necessary for land and housing security, evidence suggests land with or without housing is traded according to some form of de facto titling system, often based heavily on local governance systems (Payne et al. 2009). Formal titling and associated processes are expensive, slow and subject to dispute, even where the land is privately owned in the formal system. The informality of urban land markets that generally cater to the land and shelter needs of most low-income urban residents is as much a commentary on the infectiveness of existing formal land tenure and regulatory arrangements as it is on the flexibility and adaptability of informal land tenure arrangements. The latter are necessary to address poverty and cater for meeting 'here and now' shelter and housing needs (Jones 2012, 2016a).

By the end of the twentieth century, a shift was emerging in how to approach the persistent challenge of upgrading informal settlements, including addressing tenure regularization and the provision of sites and services. In-situ upgrading schemes became more popular as governments and development agencies aimed to limit the number of dwellers in informal settlements and slums being relocated to faraway sites. They also sought to reduce the extent of disruption to the social and economic networks of residents. Attempts at assisted in-situ upgrading implied a deeper understanding of the processes and outcomes of informality, and the dynamics of ground level urbanism permeating many informal settlements (Jones 2019a). While projects showed that 'reduced' and alternative minimum standards of urban planning could be applied, there was also a need to be more flexible in designing and implementing upgrading projects in low-income areas. Many upgrading projects became too complex because of the inclusion of many different but parallel components such as achieving land tenure security, the relocation of affected communities, promoting economic development, and the provision of sites and services. These were all under the control of the rigid conditions of modern planning and the associated project administration procedures of development partners. Implementation criteria often lacked flexibility, the latter central to communities who lived their lives by varying forms of informality and adaptability.

Furthermore, the implementation criteria used by international development agencies with the support of often reluctant governments to design and assess projects were focused on affordability, cost recovery and institutional reforms. They were based on a standard global planning template approach which was usually unsuitable for national, city and local contexts. The criteria incorrectly assumed that the principle of progressive development which characterized the upgrading of informal housing could be replicated under a planned and formal regime. It was increasingly clear that the complexities of informal settlements and the decoding of local rules, protocols and governance had not been undertaken in any depth, nor was their pivotal role understood. As a result, these projects and programs for upgrading informal settlements did not work and were slowly abandoned (Fig. 2.6).

The overall trend was that mass housing policies in many Global South countries like South America and South Africa were unable to leverage off the diversity of vibrant self-help housing and self-organization practices that underpinned the sociality and governance of informal settlements. The focus instead had been on centralized top-down delivery approaches and market-driven dynamics, with government often maintaining a strong reliance on the advice and support of the private sector. These programs failed to learn the lessons from self-help housing development and the dynamics linking incrementalism, affordability, self-help adaptation practices and timing of the renewal process. There was also a lack of flexibility in project design as well as a reliance on ownership models imported from other socio-economic groups with different contexts (Huchzermeyer and Misselwitz 2016).

Fig. 2.6 Attempts at upgrading informal settlements in North Jakarta have not been successful, and they stand side by side with formal housing. *Source* Authors (2021)

2.4 Recognizing Micro-scale Changes in Informal Settlements

In the new millennium, the scale and magnitude of the informal housing challenge has become a permanent part of the contemporary city. Two key consequences of this trend are that self-organized activities including self-help housing continue to emerge as the key generator of change, and that the term 'informal settlements' has been used in a far more constructive manner in both theoretical and professional discourses. Practitioners and researchers have explored the need to understand and better plan informal settlements and their relationship and role in the wider city. The built environment and the social dimensions of change have been increasingly analyzed as dynamic interrelated entities given informality is a strongly locally nuanced phenomenon (Suhartini and Jones 2020). Informal settlements, which in dense settings can be characterized by fine-grain and irregular morphology, are acknowledged as transforming resident housing via small-scale socio-physical alterations and adaptations (Kamalipour 2016a, b).

Self-organization has come to the fore through recognition that the process of housing transformation is typically incremental. Change occurs by dividing existing rooms for privacy or sleeping accommodation, adding a floor, inserting a balcony, reducing setbacks to add a new room or to insert external stairs to access upper levels (Kamalipour and Dovey 2019). These changes typically manifest within a set of

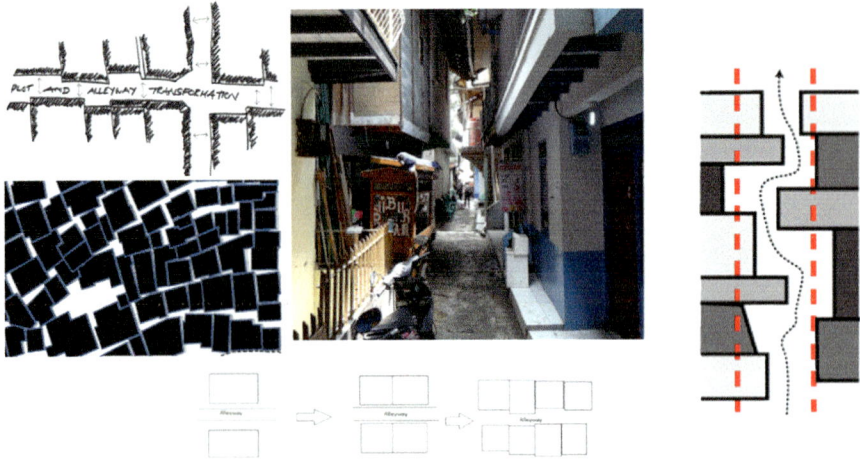

Fig. 2.7 Self-organized and incremental changes to housing have a major impact on the shape, alignment and sociality of kampung alleyways. *Source* Authors

specific 'rules', including fluid land tenure protocols, and retain the same or similar socio-material and spatial identity. The transformations by horizontal and vertical 'bottom-up' alterations often result in transgressing the 'quasi-legal' or 'legal' plot boundaries by introducing new built forms to the housing façade and subsequently changing the alleyway alignment (see Fig. 2.7). This is an ongoing process and collectively impacts on the way residents, traders and passing pedestrians engage with the new housing forms and adjoining public spaces. This includes constraints and opportunities for economic exchange and sociability (Jones 2016a, b, 2019b).

Researchers including Rapoport (1988), Dovey (2014), Jones (2021a, b), Kamalipour (2016a, b) and Kamalipour and Dovey (2019) have observed that informal settlements grow through generative processes of incremental adaptation and self-organization which meet residents' immediate needs in contrast to longer term outcomes. For example, Suhartini and Jones (2019) observed that housing in informal settlements in Indonesia resulted from unplanned adaptation of domestic space as expressed through their varying non-linear geometric forms, range of materiality and multiple construction methods, plus the development of hybrid governance arrangements. Adaptability emerged as a key process and action occurring within a framework of groups and individuals who are resilient and capable of self-organization and co-evolution across space, time and society (Jones 2021a, b; Silva 2018).

Despite these perspectives gaining ground, comparatively little attention has been given to planning and design practices that seek to better understand the impact of housing adaptation on micro-morphological and spatial patterns in informal settlements. The emphasis in research on informal settlements has been on larger scale assessments of policy, governance and existing features of the 'informal city'

(Davis 2006; Neuwirth 2004; Roy and Alsayyad 2004) rather than their micro-scale forms and processes of adaptation for housing (Dovey 2012; Dovey and King 2011; Kamalipour 2016a, b, 2017; Kamalipour and Dovey 2019; Kellett and Napier 1995; King 2011; McCartney and Krishnamurthy 2018). The physical features of informal settlements are generally not well-documented, with enclaves of housing often excluded from official local government maps and plans (Patel and Baptist 2012; Suhartini and Jones 2019). Until recently, the analysis of the unique morphological features of informal settlements has been ignored despite their potential to be utilized in designing housing upgrading programs (Duarte 2009; Dovey and King 2011; Kamalipour 2016b).

Existing methods and tools of morphological analysis in informal settlements have not addressed the self-organized and incremental housing adaptation practices. These expressions of resident's individuality include fluid property and building lines, rights of use, access to services and types of infrastructure. In dense informal settlements, microscale notions of distance (the length of space between two or more close points) and proximity (short distance of space or time) become all-important variables in determining how private and public circulation spaces are negotiated, housing form is created, and 'new' territorial boundaries are claimed. If morphology in informal settlements is concerned with identifying processes and outputs of housing transformation, then understanding housing and informal settlements as produced through self-organized fine-grain built and unbuilt micro-scale processes is critical to achieving better urban outcomes (Jones 2021b).

Although informal settlements remain being perceived as an urban policy 'problem' and subject to mixed formal planning rhetoric, policies and upgrading schemes, some cities remain accommodating and tolerant of informal settlements and slums as a means to resolve the housing challenges of the urban poor and disadvantaged. While informal settlements may be stigmatized due to their adverse physical forms and 'free aesthetics', plus mixed social capital, housing and land tenure arrangements, there has been a gradual shift by policy makers to tolerate and implicitly accept informal settlements as alternative forms of city making. Long-standing prejudices still remain due to the legality of settlements, the social status of those who live there, the challenges of incorporating practices of housing individuality into top-down plans, and the middle-class values associated with informal settlements as being 'problematic'.

2.5 Formalizing the Informal City

While the sites and services approach has long been abandoned as a singular solution for housing and services provision, various approaches spanning the bottom-up and top-down continuum of upgrading continue. Many are based on a mismatch of incremental formal and informal approaches at varying scales, with government, private sector and, importantly, informal actors being involved in varying upgrading schemes and approaches. The reflection of former upgrading approaches and their continual evolution into myriad city contexts demonstrates the complexity of the many parts that comprise the human habitat and the richness and complexity of the city. Thus, notions of 'planned, the informal and organic' coexist in the development of the city as being interlocked in a time–space–society continuum. This requires a deeper understanding of the varying historical and socio-economic contexts from which they have emerged (Suhartini and Jones 2020; Jones 2021a, b).

Long-standing assumptions surrounding the role of urban planning, architecture, and urban design in the development and application of grand visions for the city— such as the need for mainstream formal methods of financing, technical support by professional practitioners, enabling legal frameworks, and provision of basic infrastructure to settlements, blocks and households—have mixed resonance in the informal city. A key reason for the latter is that informal settlements like kampungs are one of the few settlement types in which multiple housing sub-markets can be provided for residents to buy/rent/build/invade and occupy accommodation. Thus, meeting such diverse housing needs reflects many household upgrading and renewal initiatives as characterized by physical incrementalism, hyperactive public spaces and multifunctional private spaces. Spatial changes and creative physical adaptations by individuals and households, plus land tenure issues make retrofitting infrastructure and services problematic as they do not align and comply with how modern service systems should be installed. The increasing appropriation of the city's interstitial spaces in inner city locations by residents means notions of public and private, legal and illegal are blurred and shifting, with public spaces privately used and physically taken by households and community groups (Jones 2021a, b).

As such, there is a turbulent framework of negotiable written and unwritten rules and protocols within which residents, community committees and governmental bodies work or do not work together to achieve incremental changes to meet diverse housing needs. Regardless of the nuanced informality seen in the range of kampungs in Indonesia and informal settlements generally, for example, the logic of its production and persistence remains paramount—that is, it is generated from self-organized individual and/or group social action without the support from an overarching controller. From a legal perspective, such settlements viewed through the formal lens are informal and illegal (Dhamo 2021).

Informality is a 'way of life' for many in the city (Aisayyad 2004). This term highlights Louis Wirth's key theme in his iconic book 'Urbanism as a Way of Life' which reinforced the view that urbanism reflects "complex traits making up the characteristic mode of life in cities." (Wirth 1938: 7). If we embrace urbanism as including informal settlements, slums and their dwellers and practices as a 'way of life' for the ordinary, then we need to accept what is seen by many as marginal and irrelevant phenomena instead as a rich and essential component of urbanism which defines and creates cities. Roy (2005) acknowledges this by declaring informality and informal settlements as a "mode of life" and "a mode of urbanization" which have their own "organizing logic" in a period of increasing globalisation and flows of resources and people (Roy 2005: 147) (Fig. 2.8).

Fig. 2.8 Lively neighbourhoods exist in informal settlements (kampungs) in Indonesia, where space and times for activities are contextual. *Source* Authors (2018)

There are a number of reasons why such communities engage in the process of transforming sections of the city through 'bottom-up' resident and community-led processes of self-organization. One is that governments themselves are unable to meet the backlog of demand for urban services including land, housing, water, sanitation and waste disposal, plus tenure security. In this matter, informal settlements fulfil an important shelter function which governments themselves are unable to provide. Secondly, it is acknowledged that security of tenure in myriad informal arrangements raises the prospect for both direct and indirect adaptation initiatives in terms of upgrading housing. With an upward growth of informal settlements, their formation and organization are increasingly developing through a continuum of governance arrangements from 'top-down', 'bottom-up' to 'hybrid'. In other words, a multiplicity of governance and adaptation practices and arrangements are at play at the local level in creating and sustaining such settlements (Suhartini and Jones 2014).

Despite this shift in understanding the way in which informal settlements are self-organized and managed, current conceptualizations and tools for planning of informal settlements and slums do not capture the strong relationships and dynamics between sectors, stakeholders, sociality and the physical form that drive the formation of the self-organized city. As Kamalipour (2016a) observes, urban informality is developed through a strong understanding of the processes of self-organization and incremental adaptation. Hence, it is not surprising that attempts at 'formalizing the informal' and correcting the urban disorder by realigning resident norms and values to middle-class ways of living have not been successful (Perlman 2021). The existing capacities and structures of urban governance and planning as driven by formal structures and top-down policies are generally insufficient, unable and unwilling to effectively understand, engage and integrate these alternative forms and expressions of city making. Simply, they are messy and do not align with a predisposed modernist 'one size fits all' approach that views the city as rational organism. As such, there is a wide gap between development objectives and development realities. While strategies and the literature dealing with social inclusion and slum upgrading are embellished with ideals advocating inclusion, enablement, sustainability, empowerment, capacity building and recognizing diversity, their sustained impact on practice has yet to emerge (Hamdi and Goethert 1997) (Fig. 2.9).

One key symptom of this inability to make major policy shifts is that formal planning approaches still dominate the way of resolving the 'informal settlement problem', both conceptually and in practice. Simplistic land use plans and unrealistic modernist visions are maintained as the solution to urban growth and city transformation in Asian nations including Singapore, Malaysia and Hong Kong. Questioning what constitutes notions of place and how places evolve and are governed is critical to understanding the socio-cultural milieu of society (Dovey 2009).

Fig. 2.9 The local neighbourhood governance office (RW 17) in kampung Muara Baru, North Jakarta, plays a key role in meeting the social needs of residents as well as connecting the various levels of government. *Source* Authors (2021)

2.6 Conclusion

The informal city comprising complex subsystems is an increasingly visible reality as reflected in the development of the contemporary city. The rising need for accessible and affordable housing in the context of reduced public funding and lack of interest from the private sector to provide housing for the urban disadvantaged reaffirms the necessity to ensure self-help housing and self-organized activities are promoted as a key conduit to address both national and global housing problems. The urban disadvantaged and poor are central in this challenge.

The urban disadvantaged that exist within the contemporary city are a broad spectrum of residents generally located in informal settlements and characterized by:

- Inadequate or unstable income, which translates into inadequate consumption of basic necessities.
- Inadequate, unstable, or risky asset base for individuals, households, or communities, including those assets that are important for maintaining income, coping with economic shocks, and limiting environmental hazards that can have serious health and economic costs.
- Limited or no right to make demands within the political system and receive entitlements. Frameworks do not guarantee civil and political rights, such as the right to representative government or the right to organize and receive an adequate response.
- Poor quality and/or insecure housing with inadequate provision of public infrastructure and services, which imposes a large health burden. This was and remains most evident in the consequences of the COVID-19 pandemic where social distancing and access to clean water was simply not possible for many residents.
- Inadequate protection from the law, such as for civil and political rights, workplace health and safety, pollution through environmental legislation, and from violence.
- Residing in housing located or sited on marginal and adverse environmental lands, for example, flood prone areas, waste disposal sites and under power easements.

There are strong links between these different aspects—for instance poor quality, insecure housing with inadequate provision of 'public' infrastructure and services reflects the occupants' very limited capacity to pay for housing—but it is useful to stress each of these different aspects as they highlight a different entry-point for interventions that can reduce inequities and inequalities. The contemporary city in Indonesia provides the context in which kampungs and the urban disadvantaged are recalibrated as part of the formal and informal duality, thus increasing competition and contestation over urban space through self-organized activities.

References

Aisayyad N (2004) Informality as a "new" way of life. In: AlSayyad N, Roy A (eds) Urban informality: transnational perspectives from the Middle East, Latin America, and South Asia. Lexington Books, New York, pp 7–29

Angel S (2012) Planet of cities. Lincoln Institute of Land Policy

Avni N, Yiftachel O (2014) The new divided city? Planning and 'gray space' between global north-west and south-east. Routledge

Davis M (2006) Planet of slums. Verso. Accessed from: https://doi.org/10.1111/j.1540-5842.2006. 00797.x

De Soto H (1989) The other path. Basic Books, New York

Dhamo S (2021) Understanding emergent urbanism: the case of Tirana, Albania. The Urban Book Series, Springer Nature, Switzerland

Dovey K (2009) Becoming places: urbanism/architecture/identity/power. Routledge, London

Dovey K, King R (2011) Forms of informality: morphology and visibility of informal settlements. Built Environ 37(1):11–29. Accessed from: https://doi.org/10.2148/benv.37.1.11

Dovey K (2012) Informal urbanism and complex adaptive assemblage. Int Dev Plann Rev 34(4):349–368. Accessed from: https://doi.org/10.3828/idpr.2012.23

Dovey K (2014) Incremental urbanism: the emergence of informal settlements. In: Haas T, Olsson K (eds) Emergent urbanism: urban planning and design in times of structural and systemic change. Routledge

Duarte P (2009) Informal settlements: a neglected aspect of morphological analysis. J Online Urban Morphol 13(2). Accessed from: Urban Morphology online—2009 (urbanform.org)

Fox S (2013) The political economy of slums: theory and evidence from Sub-Saharan Africa. Development Studies Institute, London School of Economics, Working Paper No. 13.

Franco D (2021) Informality and dissent—The culture of self-sufficiency of the American rural poor. In: Raimo D, Lehmann S, Melis A (eds) Informality through sustainability. Earthscan. Routledge

Hamdi N, Goethert R (1997) Action planning for cities: a guide to community practice. John Wiley, New York

Harris R (2018) Modes of informal urban development: a global phenomenon. J Plann Lit 33(3):267–286. Accessed from: https://doi.org/10.1177/0885412217737340

Hart K (1973) Informal income opportunities and urban in Ghana. J Mod Afr Stud 11(1):61–89

Huchzermeyer M, Misselwitz P (2016) Coproducing inclusive cities? Addressing knowledge gaps and conflicting rationalities between self-provisioned housing and state-led housing programmes. Sci Dir Curr Opin Environ Sustain 20:73–79. Accessed from: https://doi.org/10.1016/j.cosust. 2016.07.003

International Labor Office (1972) Employment, income and equality: a strategy for increasing productive employment in Kenya. ILO, Geneva

Jones P (2012) Managing urbanisation in Papua New Guinea: planning for planning's sake? Working Paper 33, Alfred Deakin Research Institute, Deakin University, Geelong, Australia

Jones P (2016a) The emergence of Pacific urban villages—urbanization trends in the Pacific Islands. Pacific Studies Series, Asian Development Bank (ADB), Manila. Accessed from: https://www. adb.org/publications/emergence-pacific-urban-villages

Jones P (2016b) Unpacking informal urbanism: urban planning and design education in practice. Penerbit ITB Press, Bandung, Indonesia

Jones P (2019a) The shaping of form and structure in informal settlements: a case study of order and rules in Lebak Siliwangi, Bandung, Indonesia. J Reg City Plan 30(1):43–61. Accessed from: https://doi.org/10.5614/jpwk.2019a.30.1.4

Jones P (2019b) Informal settlements and the concept of informal urbanism. In: Maryati S (ed) Understanding the informal city. Penerbit ITB Press, Bandung, Indonesia

Jones P (2021a) The role of adaptation in changing the micro-morphology of informal settlements. In: Raimo D, Lehmann S, Melis A (eds) Informality through sustainability. Earthscan, pp 180–195

Jones P (2021b) Distance and proximity matters: understanding housing transformation through micro-morphology in informal settlements. Int J Hous Pract Spec Ed Informal Hous Pract 21(2):1–27. Accessed from: https://doi.org/10.1080/19491247.2020.1818052

Kamalipour H, Dovey K (2019) Mapping the visibility of informal settlements. Habitat Int 85:63–75. Accessed from: https://doi.org/10.1016/j.habitatint.2019.01.002

Kamalipour H (2016a) Forms of informality and adaptations in informal settlements. Int J Architectural Res Archnet-IJAR 10(3):60–75. Accessed from: https://doi.org/10.26687/archnet-ijar.v10i3.1094

Kamalipour H (2016b) Urban morphologies in informal settlements: a case study. Contour J 1(2). Accessed from: https://doi.org/10.6666/contour.v1i2.61

Kamalipour H (2017) Mapping urban interfaces: a typology of public/private interfaces in informal settlements. spaces and flows. An Int J Urban Extra Urban Stud 8(2):1–12. Accessed from: https://doi.org/10.18848/2154-8676/CGP/v08i02/1-12

Kellett P, Napier M (1995) Squatter architecture? A critical examination of vernacular theory and spontaneous settlement with reference to South America and South Africa. Tradit Dwellings Settl Rev 6(2):7–24

King R (2011) Reading bangkok. NUS Press

Lehmann S (2021) The self-organising city and its modus operandi—informal urbanism and public space. In: Raimo D, Lehmann S, Melis A (eds) Informality through sustainability. Earthscan, pp 129–152

McCartney S, Krishnamurthy S (2018) Neglected? Strengthening the morphological study of informal settlements. SAGE Open Monogr 8(1). Accessed from: https://doi.org/10.1177/2158244018760375

Moser C (1994) The informal sector debate, part I, 1970–1983. In: Rakowski CA (ed) Contrapunto: the informal sector debate in Latin America. State University of New York Press.

Neuwirth R (2004) Shadow cities: a billion squatters, a new urban world. Routledge

Obermayr C (2017) Sustainable city management: informal settlements in Surakarta, Indonesia. The Urban Book Series, Springer, Berlin

Patel S, Baptist C (2012) Editorial: Documenting by the undocumented. Environ Urbanization 24(1):3–12. Accessed from: https://doi.org/10.1177/0956247812438364

Payne G, Durand-Lasserve A, Rakodi C (2009) Social and economic impacts of land titling programs in urban and periurban areas: a short review of the literature. In: Lall S, Freire M, Yuen B, Rajack R, Helluin J (eds) Urban land markets. Springer, Dordrecht. Accessed from: https://doi.org/10.1007/978-1-4020-8862-9_6

Perlman J (2021) The hill and the asphalt—a 50 year perspective on informality in Rio de Janeiro. In: Informality through sustainability. Earthscan. pp 237–253

Rapoport A (1988) Spontaneous settlements as vernacular design. In: Patton C (ed) Spontaneous shelter: international perspectives and prospects. Temple University Press

Roy A (2005) Urban informality: toward an epistemology of planning. J Am Plann Assoc 71(2):147–158

Roy A, Alsayyad N (2004) Urban informality: transnational perspectives from the Middle East, Latin America, and South Asia. Lexington Books

Rukmana D (2018) Upgrading housing settlement for the urban poor in Indonesia: an analysis of the Kampung Deret program. In: Grant B, Yang Liu C, Ye L (eds) Metropolitan governance in Asia and the Pacific Rim: borders, challenges, futures. Springer Nature Singapore. Accessed from: https://doi.org/10.1007/978-981-13-0206-0_5

Satterthwaite D (2019) Rethinking housing policies: harnessing local innovation to address the global housing crisis. UCLG World Congress, Durban, South Africa. Accessed from: Rethinking_Housing_Policies_Harnessing_l.pdf

Sengupta U, Shaw A (2019) Trends and issues in housing in Asia: coming of an age. Routledge, London, United Kingdom

Silva P (2018) Designing urban rules from emergent patterns: co-evolving paths of informal and formal urban systems—the case of Portugal. IOP Conf Ser Earth Environ Sci 158:1–10

Suhartini N, Jones P (2019) Urban governance and informal settlements: lessons from the city of Jayapura, Indonesia. The Urban Book Series, Springer Nature, Switzerland

Suhartini S, Jones P (2020) Better understanding self-organizing cities: a typology of order and rules in informal settlements. J Reg City Plan 31(3):237–263. Accessed from: https://doi.org/10.5614/jpwk.2020.31.3.2

Suhartini N, Jones P (2014) Reframing approaches to conceptualising urban governance in Melanesia: insights from Jayapura and Port Moresby. J Reg City Plann 25(2):96–114

Turner J (1976) Housing by people: towards an autonomy in building environments. Pantheon Books, New York

UN-DESA (2018) 68% of the world population projected to live in urban areas by 2050, says UN. United Nations Department of Economic and Social Affairs. Accessed from: https://www.un.org/development/desa/en/news/population/2018-revision-of-world-urbanization-prospects.html#:~:text=68%25%20of%20the%20world%20population,of%20Economic%20and%20Social%20Affairs

UNESCAP (2015) The state of Asian and Pacific cities 2015: urban transformations shifting from quantity to quality. https://www.unescap.org/sites/default/files/The%20State%20of%20Asian%20and%20Pacific%20Cities%202015.pdf

UN-Habita (2016) Urbanization and development—Emerging futures. Accessed from: https://new.unhabitat.org/global-launch-of-world-cities-report-takes-place-in-new-york

UN-Habitat (2015) Habitat 111 issue papers 22—Informal settlements. New York. May. Accessed from: https://unhabitat.org/sites/default/files/download-manager-files/Habitat-III-Issue-Paper-22_Informal-Settlements-2.0%20%282%29.pdf

Wirth L (1938) Urbanism as a way of life. Am J Soc 44(1):1–24. Access from: https://www.jstor.org/stable/2768119

World Bank (1993) World Development Report 1993: investing in health. Accessed from: https://elibrary-worldbank.org/doi/pdf/10.1596/0-1952-0890-0

World Bank (2014) Indonesia: a roadmap for housing policy reform. World Bank. Accessed from: databank.worldbank.org

Zarate L (2016) They are not "informal settlements"-they are habitats made by people. Nature Cities. Accessed from: https://www.thenatureofcities.com/2016/04/26/they-are-not-informal-settlements-they-are-habitats-made-by-people/

Chapter 3
Key Concepts in Understanding Self-organization and the Self-organized City

Abstract Cities transform through various combinations of formal and informal practices and processes resulting in a continuum of varying outcomes. In city development, informal settlements that self-organize from the bottom-up play an important strategic role by providing low and increasingly middle-income groups with affordable land, housing, livelihoods and social networks. One way to understand the self-organized city is to view them as complex unpredictable systems where cities transform through various combinations of formal and informal practices and processes. 'Top down' and 'bottom-up' practices and processes comprising relationships, flows and networks are at play. As a result, households that self-organize from the 'bottom-up' are a form of tactical and adaptive urbanism operating to a large degree outside the bounds of the formal planning system. In this setting, understanding key interrelated concepts of self-organization, complex adaptive systems, self-help housing, order and increments are fundamental to explaining a more holistic view of the emergence of informal settlements, the generative processes of incremental adaptation, and the self-organized city generally.

Keywords Self-organization · Complex adaptive systems · Self-help housing · Order · Increments

3.1 Introduction

There has been a timely shift in the twenty-first century as to how urban challenges are conceptualized, understood and planned. This has led to calls for new planning and design responses to address the complexity of modern society (Dhamo 2021). As Kostov (1993) acknowledged in the late twentieth century, the simple binary constructs of planned and unplanned, formal and informal are unable to convey in any depth the complexity of actions and stakeholders involved in the ongoing creation and modification of urban form. In a city context, the former is often characterized by a masterplan vision perpetuated by strong middle-class aesthetics and geometric plans, and overseen by a controlling authority while the latter is often organic and irregular in form and structure. This unplanned urban fabric often emerges from residents

© The Author(s), under exclusive license to Springer Nature Switzerland AG 2023   37
N. Suhartini and P. Jones, *Beyond the Informal*, The Urban Book Series,
https://doi.org/10.1007/978-3-031-22239-9_3

whose activities occur within a framework of physical constraints (or opportunities) and social protocols where residents "set their own rules" (Dhamo 2021: 90).

A basic premise of city planning and management is the need to provide stability, while also allowing for innovation and adaptability (Silva and Farrall 2016). However, the rational and modernist planning model of city planning has often been fixated on an end result that has proved inflexible and unable to cope with the growing demands from the needs of a diverse city resident population. The often-unilateral model of city development so commonly adopted does not accommodate the diverse range of urban users including their social and economic functions, accompanying urban form adaptations and diverse needs. This has a major impact on how cities are provided with land, infrastructure and services in terms of urban renewal and city edge development.

Over time, the delineation between what is planned and unplanned in the city has been based on what accords or otherwise with formal rules and regulations. The geometrically-designed city continues to be modified and organically deregulated through changing land use, demographic change and at times institutional' indifference' to enforcement of regulatory instruments such as building codes and planning rules. The irregularity of informal settlements in terms of their form and structure in a Euclidean context, plus societal preoccupation with the negative visual geometric order and aesthetics, further banishes the acceptability of what is the organic informal city (Batty and Longley 1994). As such, the legibility of the city and understanding its urban condition through the lens of its planned and organic parts and processes of intervention becomes a challenging task (Dhamo 2021). It is not surprising therefore that there has been a growing realization that we should not aim for a single model for city development with hard and fixed rules and visions, but one encompassing more dynamic models of adaptation, transformation and user needs (Silva and Farrall 2016).

One way to understand cities and urban areas is to view them as systems in which varying urban forms encompassing built and unbuilt spaces act as the conduit by which capital, people, cultures, technologies and social norms and values play out. In Indonesia, towns and cities provide the setting in which society lives, and businesses and commerce flourishes. Populations change in type, age and gender, and develop and evolve their means of communicating including social and physical adaptations. Likewise, businesses apply technological innovations to transform their aspirations, space and capital requirements which has major implications for urban form and spatial impacts.

In this way, cities transform through various combinations of formal and informal practices and processes. 'Top down' and 'bottom-up' may or may not necessarily overlap, coincide and co-evolve together. Informal settlements that self-organize from the bottom-up play an important strategic role in city development by providing low and increasingly middle-income groups with affordable land, housing and livelihoods. Notably, their communities perform critical functions in city development by providing labor for the construction, hospitality and service sectors, as well as providing cheap goods through hawking, street and market stalls (UN-Habitat 2008). Adaptability, resiliency and a complex unfolding order are key activities occurring within a framework of groups and individuals who are capable of self-organization and co-evolution across space, time and society (Silva 2018).

It is argued that a deeper understanding of the incremental practices of the urban disadvantaged in Indonesia is central to understanding how the self-organized city as expressed in kampungs adapts to current urbanization pressures. Kampungs represent complex emergent phenomenon spontaneously self-organized from the bottom-up. Their housing practices are highly organized and innovative, with the process of housing expansion and construction often being independent of official rules and regulations (Jones 2021a, b; Rosner-Manor et al 2019; Suhartini and Jones 2019). Households self-organize and respond to varying drivers of change, being a form of tactical and adaptive urbanism, which evolves and co-evolves to a large degree outside the bounds of the formal planning system. Self-governance also emerges as important in self-organization as it is the norms and values, moral codes and ethics which individuals and groups use to shape the nature of their self-organization. Therefore, understanding key interrelated concepts such as self-organization, complex adaptive systems, self-help, order and increments are necessary to explain a more holistic view of the emergence of informal settlements, the generative processes of incremental adaptation and city development generally.

3.2 The Notion of Self-organization and Key Related Concepts

3.2.1 Self-organization

Processes and practices of self-organization in informal settlements have increasingly been a topic of urban planning and design research (Kamalipour 2016a; Suhartini and Jones 2019). However, the concept is not new. Famous urbanists like Jacobs (1961) observed in her classic book *The Death and Life of Great American Cities* that cities are characterized by an organized complexity that depends to a great extent on the local interactions of residents at the grass-roots level. Such interactions and actions create unexpected outcomes and develop in the absence of centrally conceived and applied plans, evolving with the thoughts and ideas of the local agents. During the same time period, Alexander (1964) in his work *Notes on the Synthesis of Form* made the key point that cities through time were originally organized from the bottom-up. Local interaction between residents and social groups were central in defining their development path over time, and we argue that kampungs and their communities are no exception to the above processes of emergence.

The self-organization approach to understanding cities is based on the principle that the spatial order of the city is a collective result of multiple interactions between myriad plans and policies spanning the formal and informal binary and all influencing plan content and outcomes. As succinctly stated by Alfasi and Portugali (2007: 167), "No plan is capable of fully controlling a city, including those created by state and municipal planning agencies and those prepared by large firms and organization". Under the self-organization model, plans are conceived and developed within the system rather than applied externally. In this context, an essential trait of self-organization is that it occurs without the help of a central authority or controller (Dhamo 2021). Not surprisingly, unexpected outcomes driven by myriad bottom-up activities are key product of the process of self-organization. Self-organization therefore is a key process which allows cities to dynamically recalibrate their socio-spatial patterns, form and structure based on their capacity to self-organize as needs change and new determinants evolve (Alfasi and Portugali 2007; Batty 2017) (Fig. 3.1).

With many residents and households (agents) increasingly meeting their daily needs outside of formal authority and rules, it is not surprising that residents self-organize "into a collective whole that creates patterns……evolves and learns" (Mitchell 2009: 4). Because of the non-linearity of the interactions, the actors and basic institutions comprising the system tend to self-organize in the sense they facilitate local interactions via dialogue, connections and exchange. Such complex, self-organized networks typically exhibit the properties of clustering, being scale-free and forming their own nuanced system. Spontaneous patterns emerge through autonomous and self-reinforcing local interactions at the human scale, with processes of self-organization essentially creating order out of disorder (Heylighen 2008). The system or subsystem (such as kampungs) tends to self-organize with local flows

Fig. 3.1 A mural organized and sanctioned by the local community in kampung Pakualaman, Yogyakarta. *Source* Authors (2020)

and non-linear system interactions resulting in the evolution of the overall system being uncontrollable and unpredictable in its emergence. The apparent randomness and chaos of the physical structure in kampungs with unexpected outcomes, for example, are a symptom of this self-organization process (See Fig. 3.1).

Batty (2005) argues that to understand cities we must view them not simply as places located in space but as systems of flows and networks. The latter comprise the many relationships between objects and activities that compose the city and its systems. Batty (2005) further states that to understand self-organized cities, two core elements must be embraced at a fine-grain spatial scale. Firstly, there is the notion of agents being the residents and social units including institutions that constitute and forge local interactions. Secondly, there is the notion of cells which are the resulting physical and spatial structure of the city generated through local interaction and movement. In cities, self-organization is a key facilitator of urban dynamics, with planners and designers adapting and exploring the value of these autonomous processes when they deviate from plans. As Dhamo (2021) observes, "self-organization provides the conceptual basis for understanding the complexity of the always changing urban environment" (Dhamo 2021: 40). Importantly, such actions are not exclusive to informal settlements, occurring in the formal city and human systems as well.

3.2.2 Self-help Housing

A key product of self-organization in informal settlements is self-help housing, a commonplace process and outcome in the urban landscape of many developing countries (Rukmana 2018). Residents improve their housing conditions by utilizing land, finance arrangements, construction and building materials in an incremental manner. Self-help housing reveals the interaction between labor, capital and the operation of the informal economy. In other words, they secure finances and/or building materials and labor, constructing and paying for such inputs in small portions. Incrementalism as reflected in step-by-step household upgrading and adaptability is a key concept in the self-help housing process as residents improve their homes by adding and rearranging space and using different combinations of materials (Kamalipour 2016a; Suhartini and Jones 2020). The combination of architectural and design features that emerge from the unplanned combination of building materials is a good outcome of self-organization if other local sustainability goals are meet (Fig. 3.2).

The self-help (or self-build) housing movement has been a well-documented approach in the housing literature since the 1960s. These approaches have been identified as private self-help housing at the individual and collective levels, state-initiated self-help and state-assisted self-help (Sengupta and Shaw 2019). The formal adoption of self-help housing into upgrading programs was to a major extent promoted by the insights of British architect John Turner through his housing upgrading experiences in Latin America in the 1960s and 1970s. Turner and others (see Payne 2002; Turner 1972, 1976) introduced a new perspective on the understanding of informal

Fig. 3.2 Self-help housing in kampungs often involves the assistance of community members in transferring building materials via narrow alleyways. *Source* Authors (2019)

settlements, arguing that informal settlements, their communities and households all had their own rationale, innovations and creative strategies to provide and renew housing. The lack of political will, varying government-allocated resources and flexibility in funding provision to provide shelter 'fit for purpose' for varying contexts led residents to push for greater user autonomy in housing provision.

Turner argued in his publications (Turner 1972, 1976) that the poor are best positioned to improve their houses in terms of quality and size in an incremental manner as a part of everyday survival. Turner's (1968, 1977) work highlighted that self-help incrementalism was a superior approach to total redevelopment due to gains in affordability, flexibility, and encouraging community social capital. Incremental renovation and renewal of a household's buildings occurs over years and even decades. This is conditional on individual household composition and priorities, the means available and changes as dictated by the family cycle, alignment with the goals of the local institutional and goverance framework, as well as support of the broader community. Turner advocated that housing should, therefore, be considered a multi-staged process (a verb) and not a product or commodity (a noun). (See Fig. 3.3).

The intellectual influence of Turner on building upon 'bottom-up' housing practices, plus others such as De Soto who supported bringing the informal economy into the mainstream market economy, extended in research and practice across the world. It also permeated into the design of housing upgrading programs of the World Bank,

Fig. 3.3 Self-help housing undertaken in a 'step by step' and incremental manner using a variety of geometric forms and material types are hallmark traits of the housing assemblage process in kampungs. *Source* Authors (2018)

especially the sites and services programs (aided self-help). Not surprisingly, self-help housing leveraging off the processes of self-organization remains a common and traditional method of housing production throughout Indonesia, particularly in kampungs. As discussed further below, self-help schemes by their very nature of being driven by the household and community levels are unique due to the manner of their emergence and 'different co-ordination' mechanisms. Self-help housing continues to have advantages for its inhabitants in that it is tailored to both their lifecycle and household needs as well as affordability (Alananga et al. 2015).

3.2.3 Complex Adaptive Systems

Paramount to understanding self-organization is the concept of complex adaptive systems, which is founded on understanding that systems are unpredictable, open, dynamic and adaptive. Complex adaptive systems is a term that has been applied to assist in deepening our understanding of urbanism patterns generally and in informal settlements specifically (Dovey 2012). The notion of complex systems has increased in popularity in urban planning, design and architecture during the last two decades. However, in an informal settlement context, the role of self-organization remains

Fig. 3.4 Complex adaptive systems occur in types, forms and scales—this window is used for ventilation, light and public gaze, and also as the display area for a mini store. *Source* Authors (2020)

central in complex adaptative systems yet relatively understudied (Silva 2016; Silva and Farrall 2016). It is increasingly accepted that complexity theory is situated between notions of order and disorder, with complex systems neither regular and predictable, nor random and chaotic. They reflect a combination of both dimensions, being predictable in some respects, while increasingly unpredictable in others. As a result, self-organizing processes as seen in informal settlements combine many flows and parts in myriad combinations resulting in many unexpected outcomes (Fig. 3.4).

Complexity theory helps to explain that significant parts of the cities are unplanned and result from the self-organized adaptive responses of residents, groups, governance and institutions who interact in non-linear sub-systems (Silva 2016). In this context, the theoretical lens of complex adaptive assemblage as posed by Dovey (2012) is fundamental as we can see the city as comprising parts, processes and networks that are dynamic and interrelated at scales and across city stakeholders, institutions and varied planning systems. Rather than focusing on the larger-scale objects and patterns and seeking out relationships, the flows and how interactions work are key principles in underpinning assemblage thinking (Dovey 2012). The notion of complex adaptative systems is founded on the premise that "the behavior of the system depends on the unpredictable iterations between parts" (Dovey 2012: 371). This analytical lens is crucial to understanding the emergent and adaptive realities of the city 'as it is' as well as the processes of self-organization that result and drive the outcomes of complex systems, such as unexpected physical outcomes in housing change.

Complex adaptive systems are composed of many 'agents' that interact somewhat independently. They are characterized by 'emergent properties,' in which groups of interacting agents self-organize into patterns at the next larger scale. There are typically many levels of scale relationships. Rules describing scales are critical in understanding complex systems; for example, the self-similarity of the different-scaled components of a house such as a window, door, walls and floors. Similar scale—or proportion-based laws describe the spatial distribution such as the housing patterns within a kampung. Visual elements that combine and recombine as multi-scaled patterns aptly characterize much architecture. For example, a well-proportioned building generally may have windows and doors whose sizes are multiples of some basic material dimensions (stone, glass or timber for example). Groups of windows maybe designed as a visual unit, being proportional not just to the individual windows but to the whole façade. Thus, doors, windows, building mass and façade are levels of scale in a 'scaling hierarchy'. Salingaros (2000) argues that hierarchical scaling rules are as basic to complex systems in planning and architecture, as analytical rules are to physics (Fig. 3.5).

Non-linearity is a key feature of a city's complexity, with small to large plans having differing impacts and influences. For example, it does not follow that a large-scale plan or policy will have greater impact than one prepared and implemented at a local scale (Alfasi and Portugali 2007). Moroni (2015) argues that mechanisms such as plans and policies are in effect forms of control and guidance aiming to

Fig. 3.5 Individually self-organized housing units in Pakualaman Yogyakarta reflecting similar scaled windows, doors, roofing and walls are now part of a designated urban heritage area. *Source* Authors (2021)

influence the dynamics and evolution of self-organizing cities. Numerous theorists have proposed that this precarious non-linear balance is precisely what is necessary to allow processes of adaptation and self-organization to occur in cities and communities (Heylighen 2008).

3.2.4 Order

A key concept in understanding self-organization is the notion of 'order'. This term has been an important defining element in comparing formal planned towns and cities from those that are considered informal and unplanned (Jones 2017). While existing prior to the Industrial Revolution in organizing both the 'organic' and 'planned' nature of towns and cities, the concept of order has been used primarily in the modernist planning of cities. The layout of older towns and cities with little or no planned services and infrastructure struggled with the rapid growth of cities as driven by industrialization and urbanization in the nineteenth century. This generated a plethora of new issues to be addressed, including inadequate sanitation, narrow streets, dire housing conditions, air and waste pollution, poor drainage and growing levels of disease. Collectively, these required new planning orders to be implemented under the emergence of the town and country planning movement (Hall 1988). As modern planning approaches grew in the late 1800s and the early twentieth century, so too did the notion of order become a key determining factor in the planning and design of the form and function of cities. As a consequence, predictability, Euclidean geometry and the regular arrangement of objects have dominated current planning and design practices (Marshall 2008).

As detailed by Batty and Longley in their book *Fractal City* (1994), the latter explicates 'order' as a limited and constraining scope as seen in the organic and natural city. Batty and Longley (1994) determine that in the sense of Euclidean geometry the organic and irregular city "does not mean it is disordered or chaotic, but that it is not smooth" (1994: 3). In other words, just because physical form is irregular does not preclude the existence of other forms of order and regularity. Applying the notion of fractal geometry allows inquiry into functions and processes which give rise to a deeper understanding of man-made and natural patterns, including how the parts are organized in relation to the larger city. In this context, the concept of disorder is not one of negativity but rather a deeper type of order more complex in terms of relationships and connections between shape, scale and self-organized process than the planned cities of pure geometry. The principles of scale based on an initiating geometric object, plus repetition and self-similarity are essential traits for understanding the meaning of irregularity of physical form and the patterns of order contained therein.

A key characteristic of imposing a 'formal discipline' are the rules and regulations that achieve a desired formal order (Kostof 1993). In planned modern cities, the process of formalization results in standardized rules that impose hierarchical control, geometric uniformity, aesthetic 'beauty', and repetition of consistent physical styles and patterns. An explicit spatial and physical order aims to achieve certainty, including advocating development in accordance with legally approved plans and policies. A sense of permanency and desire for stability is enforced through public infrastructure, services and social harmony (Arefi 2011). Whether in new suburban greenfield estates, middle-ring or inner-city housing areas, the explicit order is reinforced by repetitive, uniform housing styles, land-use zoning and subdivisions comprising similar plot sizes, housing and setbacks. There is a conscious desire in such layouts for geometric and visual coherency as derived from a preconceived vision of what planning and design should comprise and achieve in the modern planning era. The latter approach to implementing a desired order as promulgated by governments and residents has become the domain of contemporary urban planning, management and governance in the new millennium (Fig. 3.6).

In an informal settlement context, disorder and illegality as well as the absence of physical and social order have become a central tenet underlying the patterns of informality (Dovey 2012; Jones 2017). Perceptions of what is 'order' and 'disorder' essentially emerge through processes of self-organization, organic, bottom-up, and self-made urban orders, with many such notions nuanced at the local level (Jones 2017). Informal settlements have been identified as lacking coherency, contributing to what policy makers and academics have labeled 'dysfunctional' urban patterns (Lombard 2014). Symptoms of disorder in informal settlements have been identified

Fig. 3.6 An original kampung dwelling now half-demolished is starkly juxtaposed with a new 'modernist' physical housing order. *Source* Authors (2019)

as including varying housing designs and building materials, lack of setbacks, intrusions into public space, and a lack of reticulated water, sanitation and waste disposal systems (Jones 2019a). Elements of diverse housing styles, irregular setbacks, multifunctionality, and a wide choice of new and second-hand materials perpetuate simplistic myths insinuating disorder and chaos. The diversity of a rich 'local' architecture shaped by design innovation practices, the latter central to understanding many emergent urbanism patterns, is not acknowledged. As such, these settlements and their communities are problems 'to be fixed' by introducing a 'new' order by upgrading schemes to replace the physical, visual and social chaos. There is an explicit objective in many plans of modern global cities to correct disorder in informal settlements and slums by bringing their condition into line with the current suite of 'best-practice' upgrading practices and approaches advocated by modern planning (UN-Habitat 2016). These span approaches ranging from a simple makeover to in-situ upgrading, eviction, resettlement and redevelopment, for example, involving high-rise tower blocks (Jones 2017).

In the context of clarifying types of urban order, Marshall (2008) identified two types of order: systematic and characteristic order. Systematic order is that which is readily identifiable, coherent and discernable, such as in consistent block layouts with repetitive housing setbacks, fencing heights, standards of material use, set housing styles and heights as seen in planned modern suburban and city contexts. On the other hand, characteristic order is a type of nuanced order generated by consensual and contextual social norms and values that produce their own unique form of spatial and physical layouts, such as those seen in informal settlements. Pivotal to understanding the concept of physical order is the role of scale, scaling and hierarchy. As noted, Salingaros (2000) puts forward the proposition that every urban element is formed by the grouping of sub-elements according to geometric rules that form a hierarchy at different scales. At the smallest scale, order is created by paired contrasting elements such as windows, walls, and doorways, which exist in a balanced equilibrium before aggregating at larger scales.

In the classic paper *The City is Not a Tree*, Alexander (1965) argued that planning and design have failed to achieve a deeper understanding of what gives true functionality and form to towns and buildings as they do not understand the complexity of the underlying orders. In the new millennium, Alexander (2002) takes a deeper intellectual approach to analyzing order and its relationship to complex and adaptive systems. He argues that order constitutes an understanding of the process by which objects and activities occur based on their relative positions as shaped by forces guiding their location and evolution. Alexander (2002) asserts that while understanding the multiplicity and connections of the component parts is necessary in the urban milieu, concepts of disorder emerge from our inability to comprehend the organizing processes and paths of change that form one configuration compared to another (Waguespack 2010). In other words, the built environment, whether defined as formal, informal or otherwise, is produced by orders of varying manifestation, coherency and governance. These are important notions in understanding how processes of self-organization including innovation emerge.

Fig. 3.7 In Kampung Tamansari, Bandung, spatial order and coherence is defined by similar scale, diversity of attached housing types, and similar materiality and forms within an overall 2–3 storey building envelope. *Source* Authors (2019)

Generative processes of incremental adaptation, including the rules by which spatial order is created in informal settlements, are relatively understudied and are a challenge for city planners and policymakers (Hakim 2007; Jones 2019a; Kamalipour 2016a; Suhartini and Jones 2019). The lack of explicit visible physical and aesthetic order in informal settlements leads urban planners, policy makers and the public to formulate superficial assumptions about the inhabitants of such settlements and their socioeconomic, spatial, physical and environmental conditions (Fig. 3.7).

According to Boeing (2019), spatial order in informal settlements can be clustered into two main types: visual/geometric order and social/functional order (Boeing 2019). Arguably, this typology of spatial order could also be applied to the city generally. Mikolajczyk and Raszka (2019) suggest that spatial order can be viewed constructively by considering the multi-determinants embedded in the urban fabric, including environmental, physical, economic, social and cultural factors. Importantly, this includes the role of adaptation as a form of 'spatial management' (Mikolajczyk and Raszka 2019). Moatasim (2019) highlights the importance of temporality of space, place, forms and structure to provide a greater understanding of the key features of spatial order in informal settlements. This book views elements of spatial order, both visual and social, as interconnected factors shaping self-organization and producing order (see Fig. 3.1). The order emerges from the self-organization of system parts that find their own ever-changing equilibrium, albeit temporarily, through the setting of principles and rules (Suhartini and Jones 2020).

3.2.5 Increments: The 'Building Blocks' of Micro-morphological Change

In many dense informal settlements, the main form of micro-morphological adaptation undertaken by residents to housing structures occurs through residents undertaking incremental adaptive processes. The process of incrementalism is the major consolidation process residents and households use to self-manage their socio-cultural and economic needs by altering their physical, social and economic environment (Jones 2021a). A typology of incremental design and construction in kampungs comprising six processes of 'typical increments' associated with building additions, renovation and service connections have been identified as extend, attach, replace, infill, divide and connect (Kamalipour and Dovey 2020). Depending on their placement and functionality, each increment will have a differing impact on the building, micro-morphology, access networks and open space.

In the context of increments being the physical basis of household-driven upgrading and urban renewal, residents take on multiple roles by being their own planner, designer, architect and sometimes builder. Through their own endeavours and initiatives, dwellings are renovated and extended in varying forms and structural robustness. As part of this process, housing improvements, tenure security and land acquisition often occur in the opposite hierarchical order to what occurs in the formal regulated system. While formal systems are underpinned by clear security of land title, ownership and the necessity of up-front services and infrastructure being in place or provided in a timely manner, the informal system develops through residents taking the opportunity to upgrade via increments as the need arises and the order supports such change (Jones 2016b).

In kampungs, for example, seven main types of physical increments or parts integral to housing adaptation have been identified (Suhartini and Jones 2019). These are: (i) adding floors with walls and ceilings, (ii) insertion of external access stairs, (iii) reusing built and unbuilt space through plot amalgamation or subdivision, (iv) material replacement and or attaching new services, (v) adding verandas, (vi) adding temporary or mobile form elements such as handcarts and food stands within a setback and or at the front of the dwelling in the alleyway, and (vii) changing form via practices of "interface creep" (see Fig. 3.8). Like Kostov (1993), Batty and Longley (1994) also emphasize the important role of micro scale-elements which are repeated in a similar fashion from scale to scale in city development, stressing cities are the "product of many detailed and individual decisions which have been coordinated in the small" (Batty and Longley 1994: 28).

Through multiple processes of self-organized small-scale adaptation, housing and public spaces are modified via increments, thus transitioning from one type of space and built environment to another. Multiple increments of varying materiality and functionality means myriad morphological and geometric configurations. Hence, the notion of 'free-form' micro-morphology must be seen to exist not only in the arrangement of small-scale increments of physical forms, but also in the context of

Fig. 3.8 Small increments such as floors, walls, stairs, windows, awnings and concrete building blocks are the main increments of physical change in this vertical expansion of housing in kampung Tamansari, Bandung, Indonesia. *Source* Authors (2018)

its cumulative impacts at larger scales including the block, public space areas, settlements and the wider city. Thus, modern day cities are a product of both organic and pure geometry where order is complex and hidden in self-organizing informal settlements. Smaller parts of the system interact to produce patterns, form and structure as coordinated by individuals and groups from the 'bottom-up'. They are external to top-down central oversight. As seen in formal architecture, the emerging order strongly depends on the internal socio-cultural interrelationships that comprise the processes of self-organization (Fig. 3.9).

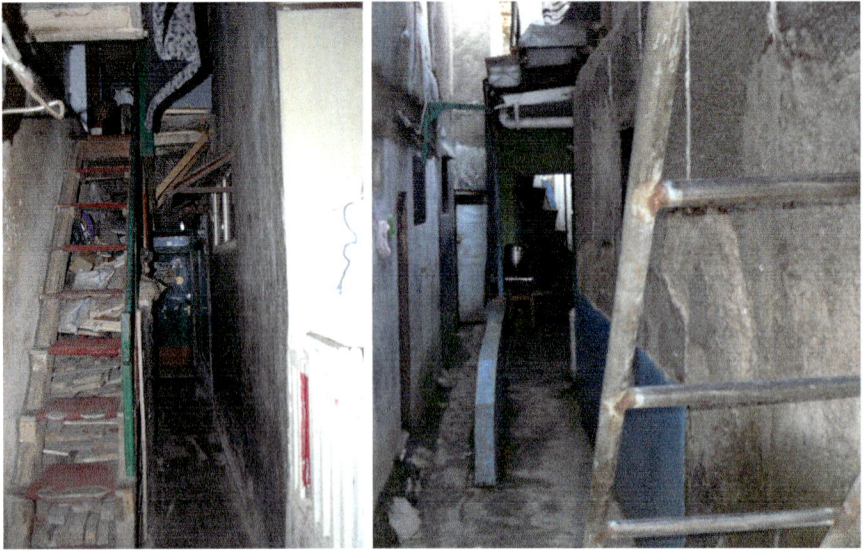

Fig. 3.9 Physical adaptation using stairs to access separate rental accommodation on upper floors is now commonplace in kampungs as demand for diverse housing sub-markets increase. *Source* Authors (2020)

3.3 Summary

A key aim of this book is to deepen our understanding of the way in which self-organization, plus the related concepts of self-help housing, complex adaptive systems, order and increments play out in shaping housing, form, structure and related activities in informal settlements. In our narrative, rules which govern self-organization are defined as a set of principles, activities, steps or phases that contribute to the development of shaping organization and/or an achievement of the prevailing spatial order. These implicit and explicit rules shape the nature of self-organization, while at the same time processes of self-organization shape and modify these rules. While both formal and informal rules may be static at times with little pressure for change, they remain the conduit by which an overarching order is achieved as set within complex adaptive systems (Jones 2019a, b). Complexity-based approaches acknowledge the city as an open system, comprising many parts that are highly adaptive to internal and external threats, and flows that cross boundaries. Parts such as informal settlements are viewed as emergent, temporal and nuanced in their respective contexts, while being integral to the functioning and understanding of the wider city (Rauws 2017; Silva 2018).

The method used in our research builds on the typology frameworks as developed by Dovey and Wood (2015), Kamalipour (2016a) and more recently, Suhartini and Jones (2019). This includes a morpho-typological approach to deconstruct and understand the relationship between spatial order, form, function and rules (Moudon

1994). The typology analysis as used in this book is set within the broader field of urban morphology and the desire for deeper knowledge regarding the transformation of the form, social and spatial structure of the city (Carmona 2010; Moudon 1994). The notion of type is central to identifying patterns of physical elements, socio-cultural rules of arrangement and types of agents that replicate themselves in built structures and the organization of land use, movement and connectivity (Scheer 2017). By studying the spatial order in parallel with self-organization, we gain insight into the socio-cultural dimensions of the types, forms, and 'hidden order' in self-help housing in kampungs. Similar traits were observed by Arefi (2011) when studying order in informal settlements in Pinar, Istanbul. The application of a typology analysis has been argued as an essential tool for better understanding the coherency and rhythm of socio-economic and physical complexity and spatial patterns embodied in built form and structure in informal settlements (Jones 2019a, b; Jones et al. 2018).

Having conceptualized the city as being emergent and unpredictable with many complex parts that are self-organized and have their own unique order, we now shift to understanding the urbanization process and its consequences in Indonesia. We seek to examine how the government has dealt with the demand for affordable housing and the planning systems and upgrading programs put in place. This includes reviewing the development of the kampung phenomena which is now extensively embedded in Indonesian towns and cities through self-organizing activities.

References

Alananga S, Lucian C, Kusiluka M (2015) Significant cost-push factors in owner-built incremental housing construction in Tanzania. Constr Manage Econ 15(33):671–688. Accessed from: https://doi.org/10.1080/01446193.2015.1090007

Alexander C (1965) A city is not a tree. Architectural Forum 12(1):58–61

Alexander C (1964) Notes on the synthesis of form. Harvard University Press

Alexander C (2002) The nature of order: an essay on the art of building and the nature of the universe. Book I, The Phenomenon of Life, The Center for Environmental Structure. Berkeley

Alfasi N, Portugali J (2007) Planning rules for a self-planned city. Plan Theory 6(2):164–182. https://doi.org/10.1177/1473095207077587

Arefi M (2011) Order in informal settlements: a case study of pinar, Istanbul. Built Environ 37(1):42–56. https://doi.org/10.2148/benv.37.1.42

Batty M (2005) Cities and complexity: understanding cities with cellular automata, agent-based models and fractals. The MIT Press

Batty M (2017) The new science of cities. The MIT Press

Batty M, Longley P (1994) Fractal cities: a geometry of form and function. Academic Press; 1st edition, Aug 17. Accessed from: file:///C:/Users/prjon/Downloads/Fractal-Cities.pdf

Boeing G (2019) Urban spatial order: street network orientation, configuration, and entropy. Appl Network Sci. Accessed from: https://doi.org/10.1007/s41109-019-0189-1

Carmona M (2010) Public places—urban spaces: the dimensions of urban design, 2nd edn. Architectural Press, Amsterdam

Dhamo S (2021) Understanding emergent urbanism: the case of Tirana, Albania. The Urban Book Series, Springer Nature, Switzerland

Dovey K (2012) Informal urbanism and complex adaptive assemblage. Int Dev Plann Rev 34(4):349–368. Accessed from: https://doi.org/10.3828/idpr.2012.23

Dovey K, Wood S (2015) Public/private interfaces: type, adaptation, assemblage. J Urbanism 8(1):1–16

Hakim B (2007) Generative processes for revitalizing historic towns or heritage districts. Urban Des Int 12(2):87–99

Hall P (1988) Cities of tomorrow: an intellectual history of urban planning and design in the twentieth century. Wiley-Blackwell, Oxford

Heylighen F (2008) Complexity and self-organization. In: Bates M, Maack M (eds) Encyclopedia of library and information sciences. Taylor and Francis

Jacobs J (1961) The death and life of great American Cities. Vintage Books

Jones P (2016b) Unpacking informal urbanism: urban planning and design education in practice. Penerbit ITB Press, Bandung, Indonesia

Jones P (2017) Formalizing the informal: understanding the position of informal settlements and slums in sustainable urbanization policies and strategies in Bandung, Indonesia. J Sustain 9(8)

Jones P (2019a) The shaping of form and structure in informal settlements: a case study of order and rules in Lebak Siliwangi, Bandung, Indonesia. J Reg City Plann 30(1):43–61. Accessed from: https://doi.org/10.5614/jpwk.2019.30.1.4

Jones P (2019b) Informal settlements and the concept of informal urbanism. In: Maryati S (ed) Understanding the informal city. Penerbit ITB Press, Bandung, Indonesia

Jones P (2021a) The role of adaptation in changing the micro-morphology of informal settlements. In: Raimo D, Lehmann S, Melis A (eds) Informality through sustainability. Earthscan, pp 180–195

Jones P (2021b) Distance and proximity matters: understanding housing transformation through micro-morphology in informal settlements. Int J Hous Pract Spec Ed Informal Hous Pract 21(2):1–27. Accessed from: https://doi.org/10.1080/19491247.2020.1818052

Jones P, Maryati S, Suhartini N (2018) The form of the informal—understanding Lebak Siliwangi, Bandung, Indonesia. Penerbit ITB Press, Bandung, Indonesia

Kamalipour H, Dovey K (2020) Incremental production of urban space: a typology of informal design. Habitat Int 98:1–8. Accessed from: https://doi.org/10.1016/j.habitatint.2020.102133

Kamalipour H (2016a) Forms of informality and adaptations in informal settlements. Int J Architectural Res Archnet-IJAR 10(3):60–75. Accessed from: https://doi.org/10.26687/archnet-ijar.v10i3.1094

Kostov S (1993) The city shaped: urban patterns and meanings through history. Thames and Hudson Ltd

Lombard M (2014) Constructing ordinary places: place-making in informal settlements in Mexico. Prog Plan 94:1–53

Marshall S (2008) Cities, design and evolution. Routledge, New York

Mitchell M (2009) Complexity—a guided tour. Oxford University Press

Mikolajczyk M, Raszka B (2019) Multidimensional comparative analysis as a tool of spatial order evaluation: a case study from Southwestern Poland. Pol J Environ Stud 28(5):3287–3297

Moatasim F (2019) Informality materialised: long-term temporariness as a mode of informal urbanism. Antipode 51(1):271–294

Moroni S (2015) Complexity and the inherent limits of explanation and prediction. Plann Theory 14(3):248–267

Moudon A (1994) Getting to know the built landscape: typo-morphology. In: Franck K, Schneerkloth L (eds) Ordering space types in architecture and design. Van Nostrand Reinhold, New York, pp 289–311

Payne G (2002) Land, rights and innovation: improving tenure security for the urban poor. Practical Action Publishing, Rugby

Rauws W (2017) Embracing uncertainty without abandoning planning: exploring an adaptive planning approach for guiding urban transformations. DISP 53(1):32–45

Rosner-Manor Y, Borghini SG, Boonstra B, Silva P (2019) Adaptation of the urban codes—a story of place making in Jerusalem. Environ Plann B: Urban Anal City Sci 1–17. Accessed from: https://doi.org/10.1177/2399808319867712

Rukmana D (2018) Upgrading housing settlement for the urban poor in Indonesia: an analysis of the Kampung Deret program. In: Grant B, Yang Liu C, Ye L (eds) Metropolitan governance in

Asia and the Pacific rim: borders, challenges, futures. Springer Nature Singapore. Accessed from: https://doi.org/10.1007/978-981-13-0206-0_5

Salingaros N (2000) Complexity and urban coherence. J Urban Des 5(3):291–316

Scheer B (2017) The evolution of urban form: typology for planners and architects, 1st edn. Taylor and Francis, London

Sengupta U, Shaw A (2019) Trends and issues in housing in Asia: coming of an age. Routledge, London

Silva P, Farrall H (2016) Lessons from informal settlements: a 'peripheral' problem with self-organising solutions. Town Plann Rev 87(3):297–319. Accessed from: https://doi.org/10.3828/tpr.2016.21

Silva P (2016) Tactical urbanism: Towards an evolutionary cities' approach? Environ Plann B Plann Des 43(6):1040–1051. Accessed from: https://doi.org/10.1177/0265813516657340

Silva P (2018) Designing urban rules from emergent patterns: co-evolving paths of informal and formal urban systems—the case of Portugal. IOP Conf Ser Earth Environ Sci 158:1–10

Suhartini N, Jones P (2019) Urban governance and informal settlements: lessons from the city of Jayapura, Indonesia. The Urban Book Series, Springer Nature, Switzerland.

Suhartini S, Jones P (2020) Better understanding self-organizing cities: a typology of order and rules in informal settlements. J Reg City Plann 31(3):237–263. Accessed from: https://doi.org/10.5614/jpwk.2020.31.3.2

Turner J (1968) Housing priorities, settlement patterns and urban development in modernising countries. J Am Inst Plann 34(6):354–363

Turner J (1972) Freedom to build; dweller control of the housing process. Macmillan, New York

Turner J (1977) Housing by people: towards autonomy in building environments. Pantheon Books, New York

Turner J (1976) Housing by people: towards an autonomy in building environments. Pantheon Books, New York

UN-Habitat (2008) Quick guides for policy makers 4 EVICTION: alternatives to the whole-scale destruction of urban poor communities. Accessed from: https://unhabitat.org/books/quick-guides-for-policy-makers-4-eviction-alternatives-to-the-whole-scale-destruction-of-urban-poor-communities/

UN-Habitat (2016) Urbanization and development—emerging futures. Accessed from: https://new.unhabitat.org/global-launch-of-world-cities-report-takes-place-in-new-york

Waguespack L (2010) Thriving systems theory and metaphor-driven modelling. Springer, London

Chapter 4
Urbanization and the Development of the Kampung in Indonesia

Abstract Indonesia is a highly urbanized and geographically diverse country guided by two interrelated planning systems, namely, spatial planning and development planning systems. Despite overall improvements in living standards, rapid urbanization has led to increasing costs for housing, services and infrastructure especially for the urban disadvantaged. A major consequence of Indonesia's urbanization process has been the inability of the planning system to keep pace with the provision of affordable housing. This systematic failing has meant that many households and residents are forced to engage in processes of self-organization and self-help housing in settlements known as kampungs so as to meet their shelter and day to day living needs. In the Indonesian context, kampungs are classed as informal settlements, being clusters of housing and support uses that are often illegally constructed on small plots using low-quality building and ad-hoc recycled materials. While originally on the edge of towns and cities, kampungs have become consumed within the expanding urban fabric and fulfil many social, physical and economic needs of the urban disadvantaged. There have been many attempts at kampung upgrading and what form this should take, the most successful being the Kampung Improvement Program (KIP).

Keywords Urbanization · Spatial planning · Development planning · Kampung · KIP

4.1 Introduction

Building on the theoretical framework outlined in Chap. 3, this chapter focuses on understanding the urbanization process in Indonesia and how national and local governments have dealt with the formal and informal planning of cities. This includes a review of the evolution and development of the kampung phenomena. Trends and patterns in Indonesian urbanization are examined, including the major growth of towns and cities, and how varying levels of government have approached the planning of urban growth. The process of formal planning is also assessed, including the hierarchy of national spatial and development plans. The latter includes the role of the kampungs, which have a long history of catering for the urban disadvantaged and lower to middle class residents seeking affordable housing through self-organization and self-help activities (United Nations General Assembly 2013).

4.2   Urbanization Trends in Indonesia—An Overview

In 2020, the urban population in Indonesia was approximately 154.2 million people, representing approximately 56.6% of the country as being urbanized (Statisca 2022). Having seen a rapid increase in urbanization since independence was gained in 1945, Indonesia's proportion of urban dwellers exceeded rural dwellers for the first time in 2011. This was also accompanied by a gradual decrease in the rural population. It is estimated that by 2045, some 220 million Indonesians or 70% of the population will reside in urban areas (Roberts et al. 2019).

While Indonesia is large and diverse, comprising some 17,508 islands, not all are densely populated or urbanized. As a result, the gains from the urbanization process have been uneven within cities and across islands. Of the islands comprising Indonesia, only 8 are home to the country's 20 most populated urban areas. Of these islands, Java Island contains 4 of Indonesia's 5 largest cities—Jakarta, Surabaya, Bandung, and Bekasi—while the city of Medan is located on Sumatra Island. Most of these cities may be considered as mega-metropolitan regions as they consume and extend into smaller towns and rural provinces (See Fig. 4.1). In 2018, 13 cities ranged between 1 and 5 million inhabitants. There were no cities with a population between 5 and 10 million, making Jakarta the largest city with almost 11 million inhabitants (Urbanet 2022) (Fig. 4.1).

Fig. 4.1 Urbanization in Indonesia reflects different modes of development interventions (formal, informal and hybrid) that create a diverse urban fabric. *Source* Rusdiana (2019)

According to the World Bank, Indonesian cities are growing faster than any other Asian cities at a growth rate of 4.1% per year (World Bank 2016). Urban growth and expansion of towns and cities has been increasingly driven by rural to urban migration in addition to a natural increase, especially in the new millennium. A strong feature of Indonesia's urbanization is that it has transgressed city administrative boundaries, having formed extended mega-metropolitan areas primarily in Java Island (Mardiansjah et al. 2021). Spatially, the development of cities in Java Island form urban corridors that stretch between big cities such as Jakarta and Bandung. Not surprisingly, the characteristics as to what distinguishes urban from rural as contained in these mega-metropolitan areas are increasingly unclear (Firman 1996). Fertile agricultural land on the outskirts of major cities and within the metropolitan regions has been developed into residential and industrial areas, confirming the fact that the rate of urban population growth and development is greatest in the suburbs rather than in the city centres.

Urban areas have also provided strong pathways for the rise of the middle class (Roberts et al. 2019). Home ownership remains high in Indonesia, being approximately 74% in urban areas compared to approximately 91% in rural areas (see Table 4.1). However, despite an overall improvement in standards of living, rapid urbanization has led to an increasing cost for housing, services and infrastructure for the urban poor, including those provided by stated-owned housing companies, particularly Perumnas (Rukmana 2018). Gains in GDP and economic growth for every 1% of urbanization have not been as high as other Asian countries. In 2015, the capacity of the national government to provide for formal housing met only 25% of the total housing needs (Mardiansjah et al. 2021).

Kampungs have traditionally been occupied by villagers and more recently the urban poor and disadvantaged, providing housing and basic infrastructure since formal housing with questionable quality is unaffordable and inaccessible (World Bank 2014). Based on a correlation analysis of the urban population and the growth of informal settlements, it has been concluded that there is a strong correlation (a score of 0.8337) between national urban population growth and the population living in informal settlements (BPS 2022). This shows that the higher the urban population growth, the higher the proportion of the population living in informal settlements. Table 4.2 shows there has been a decreasing percentage of households with access to proper urban housing in Java Island compared to the national levels between 2015

Table 4.1 % Proportion of households according to ownership status

Settlements	% Proportion of housing based on ownerships					
	Rental			Owned		
	2021	2018	2015	2021	2018	2015
Urban	14.19	15.76	14.99	73.73	71.96	73.87
Rural	1.39	1.61	1.14	90.75	89.76	91.44
Urban and Rural	8.66	9.35	8.08	81.08	80.02	82.63

Source BPS, cited 2022

Table 4.2 Percentage of households with access to proper urban housing in Java Island and Indonesia

Provinces	Percentage per province in Java and Indonesia		
	2021	2018	2015
DKI Jakarta	40	99.36	99.25
Jawa Barat	53.14	97.09	94.8
Jawa Tengah	66.47	97.4	94.96
DI Yogyakarta	85.15	99.46	98.77
Jawa Timur	66.93	96.95	95.51
Banten	60.78	96.93	93.17
Indonesia	60.9	95.7	92.85

Source BPS, cited 2022

and 2021. As Java Island has the largest urban population in Indonesia, there is a clear trend that as provincial towns and cities urbanize, there is less access to proper housing.

4.3   The Structure of Indonesia's Planning System

Indonesia is a sovereign country that implements two concurrent planning approaches, namely, spatial planning and development planning systems. Both planning systems carry out different functions and objectives in terms of delivering different public infrastructure and services, plus ensuring adequate space is allocated for land use planning. The spatial planning system as enacted by Law 26 of 2007 manages the use of land and other resources as well as planning for infrastructure. Under Law 26, the government prepares general and detailed spatial plans at the national, provincial and district levels. General plans contain land use plans and spatial structure plans addressing infrastructure needs, disaster mitigation, and the planning of future growth centres. Detailed spatial plans may or may not include kampungs and include standards and lot allocations for different types of land uses at the level of block or precinct. On the other hand, spatial structure plans address long term needs spanning twenty years of implementation. These plans may be reviewed every five years depending on the relevance of priority issues arising at that time (Suhartini and Jones 2019).

In terms of the development planning system, Indonesia is governed by Law 25 of 2004 regarding the National Development Planning System. This system sets out development programs, plans and activities to be conducted by the government at different levels. Under Law 25, governments at the national, provincial and district levels prepare development plans for the long term (twenty years or more) compared to the development of annual plans. Long term plans contain the policy framework and general priorities for development, while annual plans address programs and projects to be allocated with resources for short-term implementation. Each annual plan is required to be aligned with the priorities of the longer-term development plans. As part of this process, the preparation of mid-term plans plays a strategic role in development planning as they contain the priority social, economic and environmental objectives of the elected government leaders, such as provincial governors. In this context, the content of mid-term plans can be seen as reflecting the majority of voters' development preferences as endorsed and promoted by the potential leaders during their election campaigns (Fig. 4.2).

Ideally, resources allocated in development plans are aligned with those development themes identified in spatial plans, particularly those related to public infrastructure and service provision. Spatial plans essentially provide guidelines allocating land, water and other resources to complement and support development programs and projects. In this setting, development plans are the key tool to realize programs as enacted in spatial plans. However, it is not always the case that development plans are fully aligned with spatial plans since the preparation includes processes of public consultation with various stakeholders at different levels of government. Local aspirations, such as the direction for kampung upgrading and infrastructure priorities, colour and potentially muddy the process of development plan preparation. This results in changes to the content and prioritization of projects and programs contained in annual plans.

Fig. 4.2 Consultation for the development planning process at a city level in Jayapura. *Source* Authors (2020)

The role of community groups and NGOs are prominent in the process of development plan preparation. The community as represented by heads of RTs, RWs, and community groups like youth communities and women associations are publicly invited to nominate and discuss development issues in the initial process of plan formulation at the *Desa/Village or Kelurahan* levels. Their involvement is reduced as the planning process moves to the upper levels of government, with resources and priority issues confirmed or modified by members of the House of Representatives at the district, provincial and national levels. In summary, the planning process for managing urbanization is strongly hierarchical being a top-down movement with many layers of government bureaucracy and political deliberation (Suhartini and Jones 2019).

4.4   National Housing Policies

One of the consequences of Indonesia's urbanization process has been the major issue of providing affordable housing for the urban disadvantaged (Obermyer 2017). In 2016, the World Bank estimated that ongoing urbanization and population growth required 820,000 to 920,000 new dwelling units annually in urban areas to meet the demand for new household formation. With the private sector contributing approximately 400,000 dwelling units annually, plus only 150,000 to 200,000 dwelling units delivered by the public sector, there is a demand shortfall estimated to be between 220,000 to 370,000 dwelling units. As a result, households are forced to resort to self-organized and self-help solutions to meet their shelter needs, with these activities invariably occurring in kampungs. As affordable housing demand increases each year, there is a massive cumulative housing deficit estimated to range between 3.5 and 17 million units depending on which criteria are used (World Bank 2016).

The majority of the urban poor are concentrated in the highly urbanized and densely populated Java Island, the latter accounting for in excess of 66% of Indonesia's low-income population. The responsibility for housing policies and programs is primarily shared between the Ministry of Public Works and the Ministry of Public Housing. The National Planning Agency (BAPPENAS) has overarching responsibility for the coordination and integration of housing policies and their alignment with National Development Plans (United Nations General Assembly 2013). The main law regulating housing provision in Indonesia is contained in Law 1 of 2011 regarding Housing and Settlements. The law stipulates provisions for housing types as well as resource allocation, including directions for the provision of housing by local governments. However, the reality is that the local governments do not have the skills or resource capacity to address affordable housing needs on any major scale. Not surprisingly, Law 1 was followed by the enactment of operational regulations, including support for in-situ upgrading at the local level (Rukmana 2018).

In terms of increasing the affordability and access to both housing and land, Indonesia has applied different types of policies and programs (World Bank 2014). These are summarized below:

a. "Slum clearance and relocation into rental housing" with the key aim to improve housing quality by evicting communities from their current settlements to new locations. Many of these development programs commenced in the late twentieth century and focused on moving residents into rental housing. Negative impacts included reducing household incomes and splintering social networks and communities.

b. "Land consolidation/readjustment programs" which has been applied since 1981 in 25 provinces. These land programs are problematic and slow, constrained by issues with disputed and contested land ownership and subsequent registration arrangements.

c. "In-situ upgrading", namely the Kampung Improvement Program (discussed further below) and subsequent program reiterations. This Kampung Improvement Program as initiated in 1969 has been developed and refined over several decades. This includes the Kecamatan Development Program (KDP, launched 1997), the National Program for Community Empowerment (PNPM, launched 1999) and the Neighbourhood Upgrading and Shelter Sector Project (NUSSP, launched in 2005). All these programs had a common goal to improve urban slum neighbourhoods and access to appropriate housing for low-income households.

d. "Rusunawa and Rusunami" which commenced in the 1980's and aimed to provide both rental and privately-owned public vertical housing for low-income employees via initiatives from the Ministry of Public Housing and Ministry of Public Works.

e. The concept of "land banking" which emerged in the agrarian land reforms of the 1960's and has now shifted to acquiring and developing land for public uses including affordable housing.

f. National programs on water, sanitation, and drainage linked to slum upgrading. Known as 'Kotaku' or "cities without slums" (Kotaku 2020), the ambitious program was enacted in the National Medium Term Development Plan (RPJMN) of 2015–2019.

Generally, the policies embodied in Indonesia's planning laws have advocated for a 'rational and normative' approach to address the multitude of urban development issues that arise. These include economic, social, environmental, infrastructure and service issues as based on growth trends and statistics. Middle and upper-class neighbourhoods have been built according to Indonesian codes and legislation, most of which have Dutch origin. However, the remainder of Indonesian towns and cities have developed primarily through a range of informal processes, the latter often overlain and leveraging off former planned initiatives. As the urban populations have increased, land invasions, illegal subdivisions and the gradual expansion of non-planned settlements including kampungs have produced unregulated settlements with high densities, a lack of proper infrastructure and minimum public facilities (Obermyer 2017).

In terms of upgrading kampungs and other informal settlements, two formal approaches exist in Indonesia. Firstly, total redevelopment is an approach where existing kampungs and informal settlements not classified as kampungs are demolished and the inhabitants resettled to other locations, often peri-urban areas. Livelihoods, social networks and community capital are threatened, eroded and disconnected. On the other hand, there is the in-situ upgrading approach as seen in the various reiterations of the Kampung Improvement Program. This approach involves developing the existing informal settlements in their current location. Contextual issues of local importance to residents including housing quality, land tenure, infrastructure and social services (for example, provision of mosques, water, sanitation and electricity) have been addressed with varying levels of success. While the practice of resettlement of kampung dwellers to greenfield locations continues, there is a growing movement questioning existing resettlement rationale and advocating more challenging in-situ upgrading approaches (Dovey et al. 2019) (Fig. 4.3).

Current upgrading policy in Indonesia is increasingly anchored on the principles underpinning the in-situ approach, with an increasing focus on recognizing self-organization and building on resident initiatives to improve their situation in both approaches. In Indonesian cities and towns, they are shaped as much by informal processes as by formal processes, with official estimates in 2013 estimating 80% of housing provided in Indonesia emerged through informal self-organized systems. Much of this self-help and self-regulated housing has occurred in kampungs, thus allowing the national government to externalize the cost of providing low-cost affordable housing for the urban disadvantaged and lower middle class (United Nations General Assembly 2013). Those residents most impacted are low and middle-income

Fig. 4.3 Self-organized and self-help housing in kampungs has not yet been able to be formally upscaled and mainstreamed on a consistent basis in Indonesian housing policies. *Source* Authors (2020)

urban households, thus contributing to the rapid vertical and horizontal expansion of kampungs. In this context, the combination of rapid urbanization, increasing urban population densities, rising land and housing prices and high poverty rates pose major challenges in attaining the right to adequate urban housing in Indonesia (World Bank 2014).

4.5 Understanding the Evolution and Role of the Kampung

The term "kampung" is derived from the Malay and Indonesian language and was traditionally used to describe a system of village settlements (Anindito et al. 2018; Setiawan 2010). In Javanese tradition, kampung refers to a village or urban community, being a settlement or compound of housing containing a certain ethnic community (Azamil 2018). Coupled with the use of kampung in mainstream Bahasa usage is the term "kampung kota", which was introduced by the Dutch Colonial government through its kampung upgrading programs. Kota is originally a Malay word and in Bahasa means a "fort", "village", "town", or a "city" (and in Sanskrit equates to "a fortified place"). The linking of the term kampung with the meaning of kota ensures each kampung is connected by name to the contextual characteristics of the kampung including locality, ethnicity, how they were formed, and the type of residents (Milone 1993; Widjaja 2013).

The development of kampungs as embedded in the fabric of Indonesian towns and cities can be traced back to varying periods of colonization and more recently, the process of urbanization. For the colonizers and other incoming migrants who came to work in plantations, offices, factories, sugar mills and government in the eighteenth and nineteenth centuries, housing was a basic necessity to be fulfilled. There was also the need to house and/or relocate the indigenous population (natives) whose lands had been acquired and taken by the colonizers. Primarily located on the city edge, housing for the indigenous population and low-skilled migrant workers such as the Chinese and Arabs was provided in settlements known as kampungs (Tunas and Peresthu 2010; Widjaja 2013). The kampungs were essentially enclaves that contained different ethnic minorities whose social and physical transformation became accepted and tolerated as a home for the urban disadvantaged and lower income groups (Rukmana 2018). While the concept of a dual city was officially rescinded after independence, the spatial legacy of kampung settlements as embedded in the urban fabric can be observed in all Indonesian towns and cities.

While the Dutch had traded with the Javanese since the 1500's, the establishment of the Dutch Colonial Government in 1810 saw a formal policy introduced to separate kampungs (*Indlandsche Gemeente*) from other settlements as occupied by wealthier economic migrants (*warga priyayi* or *stads gemeente*). In the original Dutch capital Batavia before being renamed Jakarta by the Japanese in 1940, there were two basic types of settlements: the European planned settlements and kampungs (Van der Molen 1993). The European settlements were inhabited by the Dutch and other 'well-to-do' residents of European origin, including senior civil servants. Conversely, kampungs were considered unplanned, located beyond the official city boundaries, and occupied mainly by indigenous population, 'less well-to-do' residents and foreign migrants. The latter included Europeans, Chinese, Indians and Arabs.

Sullivan (1986) argues that that all types of residential areas in colonial Yogyakarta in the nineteenth century were called kampungs regardless of their quality, socio-economic status and ethnic association. It should be noted that in the case of Bandung, kampungs in one form or another as settlements of ethnic enclaves had existed since the era of Tatar Priangan in the mid-fifteenth century and earlier. This is historically important as it is often assumed that kampungs were only established during the era of Dutch Colonialization from 1810. However, the reality is that for most Indonesians the Dutch colonial domination existed for approximately 350 years, with policies of housing segregation applied by the Dutch during this time (Gultom 2018: Widjaja 2013).

The passing of the Dutch Decentralization Law in 1903 led to the formation of European urban communities under a local government entity similar to *gemeenten* (municipalities) in the Netherlands. The law also formalized kampungs as settlements to accommodate the indigenous population and less affluent ethnic migrant groups. The jurisdiction of these municipalities came under the control of a mayor. However, they did not reach and encompass all *desa* (villages) including those villages on the peri-urban edge and more distant rural villages inhabited by the indigenous people. The latter were administered by *inlandsche gemeenten* (indigenous municipalities) under the jurisdiction of the Regent *(Bupati)*. In contrast to the rural *desa*, the urban kampungs had no or minimal links with agricultural land as their lands were used entirely for residential and other urban purposes.

The urban kampung continued emerging as a homogenous or mixed neighbourhood for impoverished Europeans, foreign Oriental ethnic groups and the indigenous population. During the era of Indonesian independence, kampungs increased in number because of the Bandung Lautan Api (Bandung Sea of Fire). This was the deliberate burning of much of the southern side of Bandung by retreating Indonesian Republican troops during the Indonesian National Revolution of 1945–1950. The second driver of an increased number of kampungs was due to the tragedy of Darul Islam/Tentara Islam Indonesia (DI/TII), which was an Islamist group that fought for the establishment of an Islamic state in Indonesia. Established in 1942 by a group of Muslim militias, it was coordinated by a charismatic radical Muslim politician, Sekarmadji Maridjan Kartosoewirj, and only recognized Sharia law (Hamidah et al. 2017) (Fig. 4.4).

Evolving primarily during the era of Dutch Colonialization in the nineteenth century and at the time of Independence in twentieth century, kampungs have now became known as settlements for indigenous and non-indigenous populations. They have become physically and socially entrenched as an inseparable part of Indonesian towns and cities. Kampungs are in many locations including settling on and adjacent to riversides, waterways, railway corridors, reservoirs, centers of economic activity and at the edges of towns and cities (Rukmana 2018; Voskuil 1996). The earlier established kampungs had their unique characteristics which included ethnic

Fig. 4.4 Kampungs in Indonesia have been well established urban settlements prior to colonialization, reflecting a mix of local and foreign influences on physical form, land use and structure. *Source* Authors (2021)

grouping policies as directed by the Dutch colonial regime. The result of this policy meant that many kampungs acquired their kampung name based on the dominant migrant groups who established the settlement.

In Jakarta, for example, the original kampungs can still be found as represented in district names such as Kampung Melayu (kampung of the Malays), Kampung Bugis (Buginese village), Kampung Cina (also known as Pecinan, which refers to a Tionghoa village), Kampung Bali (kampung of the Balinese), Kampung Ambon (Ambonese village), Kampung Jawa (Javanese village), Kampung Arab (Arab village) and Kampung Banda (kampung comprising people from Kepulauan Banda) (Gultom 2018). Spatial regulations by the colonial rulers created separate and distinct residential settlements and local populations. As such, these early kampungs which still exist today can be seen as reflecting instruments of power, colonial domination and socio-cultural control at that point in time (Anindito et al. 2018). The kampung phenomena has now become an inseparable part of growing urban areas, with Wilhelm (2011) estimating that in Jakarta some 60% to 70% of the population resides in kampungs.

Kampungs may vary according to location, age, developmental drivers and processes and changing demographic profile. Different types of self-organized housing and their community governance display different characteristics and typologies. Each has its own spatial, physical and social relationship with the city, with some being isolated while others are more integrated (Suhartini and Jones 2019). Often densely populated, self-built housing with low service provision contains precarious housing that varies in quality, size and process. For example, many kampungs in Jakarta, which boasts the largest metropolitan area in Southeast Asia, are considered slums. The latter are kampungs classified by government as substandard, being forms of shelter illegally-constructed and built from makeshift materials. They are often sited in adverse environmental settings (Rukmana 2018). The poor and lower middle-income residents dominate the demographic profile of Jakarta's unregulated kampungs which are in both the core and the peripheries of the Jakarta Greater Metropolitan Area (Rukmana and Ramadhani 2021). Importantly, kampungs benefit from the wider city and the city benefits from them via labour, specialist low-cost skills and services of the informal economy. However, kampungs still share common defining urban features, most notably high density, poor living conditions, minimal efficient infrastructure and public facilities, questionable land tenure status and mixed demographics (Jones 2020).

In contemporary Indonesian towns and cities, kampungs are scattered throughout their jurisdictions and create a patchwork of poverty and disadvantage. Settlements with minimal or no infrastructure combined with poverty sit alongside the most fashionable business and housing districts, such as in Bandung, Surabaya and Greater Jakarta. The poorest of kampung dwellers are marginalized urban residents who illegally secure their plot and construct their dwellings on state land including disposal sites, riverbanks, or on private vacant land (Rukmana 2018). Not surprisingly, words such as *permukiman kumuh* meaning 'dirty settlements' or 'slums' are often used in Indonesian Bahasa language to describe the condition of kampungs. This occurs despite newer dwellings containing 'modern' design elements like permanent materials adjoin houses developed in the traditional Sundanese style in many kampung neighbourhoods. As a result, kampungs have become a unique form of settlement whose variety is expressed in organic and non-linear physical patterns whilst simultaneously being an embodiment of history, social and cultural norms (Widjaja 2013) (Fig. 4.5).

Kampungs are mostly located near sources of livelihood, thus creating specific types of employment opportunities, mostly informal (Obermayr 2017). Residents use their houses for various economic activities, such as mini-stores, salons, kindergartens, boarding houses (often for university students) or household-scale industries. These are often located adjoining major and minor alleyway patterns. The local kampung governance systems have often co-evolved with the Indonesian systems of local governance centred around the key local level administrative units of RTs and RWs (Suhartini and Jones 2020). With limited government service provision, residents often access basic services through self-organized connections or unregulated service providers (United Nations General Assembly 2013).

There are three types of land ownership in Indonesia within which kampungs and their households operate: formal, semi-formal, and informal tenure (Reerink and van Gelder 2010). Formal tenure includes landowners who have legitimate ownership

Fig. 4.5 Declining kampung condition is common as poverty and housing affordability issues rise, with formal sanitation provision often funded by state enterprises for communal uses. *Source* Authors (2020)

as acclaimed by the national Agrarian Law of 1960. These take a variety of forms, including use rights (*hak pakai*) and the right to build (*hak guna bagunan*), in addition to freehold ownership (*hak milik*) (Leitner and Sheppard 2017). Semi-formal tenure is defined by permits registered by customary law. Informal tenure includes tenants who occupy government land without official permission (squatters), while informal agreements to occupy land and buildings are those made with owners (legitimate or otherwise). However, they are not recognized or registered by the formal system. The latter are registered at a local district administrative level of Kelurahan and importantly do not represent formal ownership. These divisions of ownership have the potential to obfuscate varying notions of legality and increase the uncertainty of land tenure status on kampung plots. The result is that taking and using land and extending housing by small increments where no enforcement exists has become an acceptable and tolerated practice by kampung residents and households (Suhartini and Jones 2019).

Kusno (2019) suggests that kampung residents do not formalize their land tenure for two reasons. Firstly, formal tenure does not provide permanent security from the state who can dispossess ownership of land for development projects. Secondly, a semi-formal 'flexible' form of tenure is more affordable than formal tenure which demands a higher fee for processing and ensuring regulations are met. The varying legal status of land and questionable land tenure status on some plots is exacerbated by a culture of informal land-sharing, land-taking and subdivisions within and outside of families. With increasing population growth and pressure for affordable housing, this practice has increased from one generation to the next. As such, semi-formal and informal land tenure, plus the strategic location of some kampungs makes them a target for formal renewal by the private sector and government (Jones 2017).

As urban centres in Indonesia continue to expand due to rural–urban migration, natural population increases and wider urbanization pressures, many rural kampungs continue to be consumed within the urban administrative boundaries. Like existing kampungs located in popular inner-city strategic locations, middle-ring suburbs and urban edge areas, the kampungs on the periphery of the city become part of the wider urban area. In essence, many kampungs remain remnants of the original *desa* (villages), being absorbed by the expanding city where self-organization is a commonly accepted practice to solve housing challenges and meet daily needs. Kampungs emerge over time as a collective of mainly permanent houses of varying quality reflecting ingenuity and innovation to adapt in space and time to the changing needs of households. Most dwellings in these spontaneous informal settlements were built and are now occupied by the urban poor and disadvantaged (Rukmana 2018).

Many urban local government authorities do not have the political will, financial resources and know-how to make any substantial inroads to the adverse conditions of their kampungs. The messy land registration system, smallness of plots and the irregularly-aligned alleyways also make it difficult to officially acquire land for public uses. Major formal upgrading requires long term planning, large amounts of capital, and political consensus whilst managing the different development agendas and interests of stakeholders (Tunas and Peresthu 2010). Given the complexity of the challenges at hand, governments including RTs and RWs seem content to let the urban disadvantaged live in their own self-organized housing and communities given the important role they play in meeting affordable housing needs. This occurs alongside recent efforts of the private sector (often with municipal governments) to target kampungs for the middle and higher ends of the housing market to ensure the highest possible profit (Jones 2017).

There have also been settlements emerging adjacent to kampungs. These typically evolve into slums or squatter settlements and are organically built on land unsuitable for residential areas. These locational patterns are often defined by marginal lands alongside riverbanks, flood ways and railway corridors, as can be seen in the Jakarta metropolitan area (Tunas and Peresthu 2010; Widjaja 2013). However, managing these types of informal settlements is problematic because Indonesian regulations recognize these slums as unplanned informal settlements. This means that they receive little formal support in city plans and are excluded in national programs such as Kotaku (2020). This system of classification leads NGO programs to improve the condition of slum areas to minimum living and health standards, regardless of whether these settlements have socio-economic and historical contexts designating them as kampungs.

As an integral part of the city fulfilling the many needs of the urban poor and disadvantaged, kampungs remain at the centre of public debate. Issues of their legality, physical and socio-economic conditions, and appropriate forms of redevelopment, including the relocation of kampungs located in sensitive environmental lands, are recurrent themes. All these issues have received various responses from the public and private sectors. For example, since 1998, forced evictions in Jakarta have primarily targeted 'illegal' kampungs in the name of flood mitigation programs (Leitner and Sheppard 2017). In Jakarta where the capital is built on alluvial lowlands, kampungs have a long history of abutting the twelve major rivers which traverse the floodplains and are subject to annual flooding. In recent years, 'river normalization' programs have become the norm resulting in kampung evictions and resident displacement (Leitner and Sheppard 2017).

Like other Indonesian cities, Jakarta has been transformed and branded as a 'world-class city', with many kampungs located in valued inner-city locations being seen as a barrier to modernization. A key challenge for real estate developers targeting kampungs in Indonesia has been to convert informally settled lands into high-rise housing and retail assets suitable for the formal market. This includes demands for housing from a growing middle class. An example can be seen in Bandung, where kampungs have had red letters painted on their external walls to indicate that the residents are squatters, whether they are or not. This increases resident anxiety as to their uncertain future (Jones 2017). With question marks hanging over the legality of many kampung plots and residents wary of threats of court action from private developers who are often supported by government, developers pursue kampung dwellers to sell their lands below market value. While some residents are offered subsidies and relocation to housing that are more *layak* (adequate), the fear of eviction for kampung dwellers is significant. Residents must consider the impact on their income, livelihoods, socialization and the socio-cultural fabric which has historically protected their lifestyles and facilitated adaptation to change (Leitner and Sheppard 2017). In this context, understanding the important place and role of kampungs that have emerged through processes of self-organization by its inhabitants remains central to urban policy and future management of Indonesian towns and cities (Fig. 4.6).

4.6 The Importance of the Kampung Improvement Program (KIP)

Given the centrality of kampungs in Indonesian society, it is not surprising that attempts to improve the condition of kampungs are not new. The Dutch Colonial Government issued policies related to the planning of cities (*Gemeente*), the provision of housing for Dutch residents and improvement programs for native villages and kampungs. During the Old Order, the government established three different institutions that funded the construction of public housing and undertook research to examine the best options for low-cost housing. In 1939, initiatives to improve the condition of the kampungs were commenced by the Dutch Colonial Government and were based on the principle of integrating the kampung and their associated informal sector activities with the formal sector (Wertheim 1958). Following Indonesian independence, the concept of kampung improvement was seriously pursued, and

Fig. 4.6 Inner city kampung dwellers in Bandung are under the threat of eviction from new forms of residential development. *Source* Authors (2018)

by 1968 the concept was revitalized through the successful Kampung Improvement Program (KIP). Globally recognized as the world's first slum and informal settlement upgrading scheme, the KIP name derives from the Husni Thamrin kampung upgrading project carried out in Jakarta by the Provincial Government of Jakarta commencing in 1969, and then applied to Surabaya (World Bank 2014). After receiving international recognition, including the development of project financing options, the KIP was extended between 1972 and 1992 to all major towns and cities in Indonesia and was funded by the World Bank (Hamidah et al. 2017).

The early iterations of KIP emerging in the 1970s were based on a 'site and service' concept aiming to reduce poverty, increase the affordability and quality of housing, and provide basic infrastructure and facilities. There were two key objectives: to upgrade housing to ensure the retention and improvement of the existing housing stock; and to provide serviced sites on which low-income families could construct new housing using self-organized and self-help help methods (World Bank 2014). By providing land and basic services, plus renewing existing housing, it was envisaged that the costs of construction would be significantly reduced given they would be provided 'in kind' by households and community. Under this approach, it was expected that KIP could reach out to twice as many households as before. The content of the programmes would differ from one kampung to another depending on local circumstances. However, central in all projects was improvements to housing, access to vacant land where possible, plus upgrades to roads, drainage, sanitation, solid waste management and water supply. Schools and local health clinics were also constructed (Tunas and Peresthu 2010).

Due to its centrality and association with the KIP, the term kampung has gained mainstream use by the Indonesian government and public in the new millennium. In contrast to early Dutch kampung projects (*Kampoeng verbetering*) that aimed to protect the settlements of Dutch citizens from infectious diseases emanating from native villages, the revamped KIP of the late twentieth century sought to raise the dignity and wellbeing of the indigenous disadvantaged population primarily in an urban setting. From its humble beginnings centred on modest gains in village improvement, the KIP has developed into the Integrated City Infrastructure Development Program (P3KT), the Village Settlement and Housing Program (P3D) and subsequent program iterations. These have all focused on the provision of affordable housing and environmental infrastructure, empowering skills and cooperation at all levels, and increasing household income through greater livelihood options. In the modern reform era, the government has stipulated a 1:2:3 housing provision, thus requiring in the construction of one luxury housing unit that it be accompanied by two medium-sized housing units and three basic housing units (Rukmana 2018). While the uptake has been mixed, the rationale for this policy was to encourage the private sector to participate in providing low income and affordable housing. In addition to encouraging private sector participation, the government began to refocus on self-help housing programs in the form of financial assistance and encouraging partnerships (World Bank 2014).

In summary, Indonesia has globally led the way in some of the most innovative and comprehensive slum upgrading programs as focused on the vast array of different kampung settings. The KIP and its program iterations all leveraged the concept of *Tribina*, that is, the integrated physical, social and economic improvement of kampungs. These were essentially area development schemes and made significant gains. Over time, program reviews indicated that in-situ upgrading in KIP was seen as the best way to address the structural causes underpinning the emergence and growth of kampungs and slums. The KIP linked basic services in kampungs to broader urban development, whilst leaving housing development as supply and demand-driven and founded on self-help practices. However, as a top-down driven program where individual housing and area development remained supply-driven, it was scaled back as central government interest and support vacillated (World Bank 2014). The implementation process was characterized by contradictions and inconsistencies between the legally-prescribed in-situ approach and the political rhetoric. The latter has tended to endorse direct and sometimes repressive approaches to 'formalize the informal' and eliminate kampungs, with those in inner city locations being particularly at risk (Jones 2017). This contradictory approach represents a typical paradox of "progressive policy" on the one hand, and retrogressive politics on the other (Pithouse 2009).

The timeline on main policies and programs influencing Indonesia's housing sector is summarized in Fig. 4.7.

History of development of policies and programs in the housing sector:

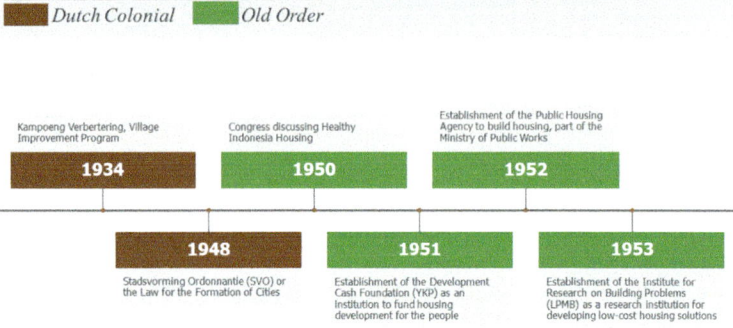

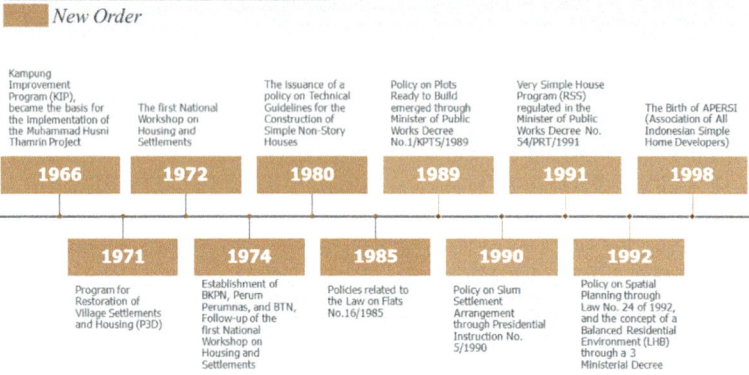

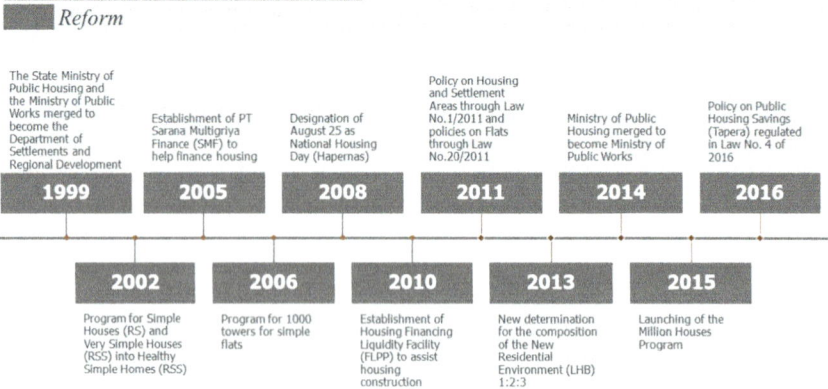

| | Dutch Colonial | | Old Order |

Kampoeng Verbertering, Village
Improvement Program

Congress discussing Healthy
Indonesia Housing

Establishment of the Public Housing
Agency to build housing, part of the
Ministry of Public Works

| **1934** | **1950** | **1952** |

| **1948** | **1951** | **1953** |

Stadsvorming Ordonnantie (SVO) or
the Law for the Formation of Cities

Establishment of the Development
Cash Foundation (YKP) as an
Institution to fund housing
development for the people

Establishment of the Institute for
Research on Building Problems
(LPMB) as a research institution for
developing low-cost housing solutions

History of development of policies and programs in the housing sector:

| | New Order |

Kampung
Improvement
Program (KIP),
became the basis for
the implementation of
the Muhammad Husni
Thamrin Project

The first National
Workshop on
Housing and
Settlements

The issuance of a
policy on Technical
Guidelines for the
Construction of
Simple Non-Story
Houses

Policy on Plots
Ready to Build
emerged through
Minister of Public
Works Decree
No.1/KPTS/1989

Very Simple House
Program (RSS)
regulated in the
Minister of Public
Works Decree No.
54/PRT/1991

The Birth of APERSI
(Association of All
Indonesian Simple
Home Developers)

| **1966** | **1972** | **1980** | **1989** | **1991** | **1998** |

| **1971** | **1974** | **1985** | **1990** | **1992** |

Program for
Restoration of
Village Settlements
and Housing (P3D)

Establishment of
BKPN, Perum
Perumnas, and BTN,
Follow-up of the
first National
Workshop on
Housing and
Settlements

Policies related to
the Law on Flats
No.16/1985

Policy on Slum
Settlement
Arrangement
through Presidential
Instruction No.
5/1990

Policy on Spatial
Planning through
Law No. 24 of 1992,
and the concept of a
Balanced Residential
Environment (LHB)
through a 3
Ministerial Decree

History of development of policies and programs in the housing sector:

| | Reform |

The State Ministry of
Public Housing and
the Ministry of Public
Works merged to
become the
Department of
Settlements and
Regional Development

Establishment of PT
Sarana Multigriya
Finance (SMF) to
help finance housing

Designation of
August 25 as
National Housing
Day (Hapernas)

Policy on Housing
and Settlement
Areas through Law
No.1/2011 and
policies on Flats
through Law
No.20/2011

Ministry of Public
Housing merged to
become Ministry of
Public Works

Policy on Public
Housing Savings
(Tapera) regulated
in Law No. 4 of
2016

| **1999** | **2005** | **2008** | **2011** | **2014** | **2016** |

| **2002** | **2006** | **2010** | **2013** | **2015** |

Program for Simple
Houses (RS) and
Very Simple Houses
(RSS) into Healthy
Simple Homes (RSS)

Program for 1000
towers for simple
flats

Establishment of
Housing Financing
Liquidity Facility
(FLPP) to assist
housing
construction

New determination
for the composition
of the New
Residential
Environment (LHB)
1:2:3

Launching of the
Million Houses
Program

Fig. 4.7 Timeline of the Main Policies and Programs influencing Indonesia's Housing Sector. *Source* Adapted from: https://perumahan.pu.go.id/article/101/sejarah

4.7 Summary

Set within the context of rapidly increasing urbanization in Indonesia, kampungs have evolved through processes of self-organization including self-help housing. Self-organization defines their nuanced informality and unexpected outcomes, including house siting, irregular block patterns, mixed use, sociality and the labyrinths of alleyways which characterize their form, structure and layout. Kampungs have become an essential part of Indonesian urban fabric, having evolved as a major conduit in providing low-income housing through systems of self-organization. They nurture and sustain the economic development of the city through labour supply and consumption whilst contributing to the socio-cultural order and fabric of wider Indonesian society (United Nations General Assembly 2013).

In acknowledging the long-standing role of the kampungs in providing affordable land and housing, the Indonesian planning system grapples to find a balance between what formal development and stability should be and look like as expressed in laws, policies and institutions, whilst allowing adaptability and innovation as expressed in self-organized urban kampungs on the other. As a phenomenon in all Indonesian towns and cities, self-organized activities are generated in kampungs where family connections and empathy to diverse kampung demographics and socio-cultural norms and values are key elements defining social networks. As Tunas and Peresthu (2010) observe, practices of self-organization and self-help housing production leverage the social capital of residents to meet the shelter needs of the urban poor and rising urban middle class in Indonesia. As a key determinant of city form and structure, what does this self-organization look like? What does it comprise and how do the processes of self-organization occur?

These fundamental questions are explored in the case studies and their respective analysis as set out in Chaps. 5, 6 and 7. The emphasis in the analysis of the case studies is to unpack material and non-material transformation and change in kampungs as products and assemblage of everyday practices of multiple actors, institutions, activities and processes. In the three case studies, we examine their history, socio-economic characteristics, governance system, morphological evolution, and adaptation strategies (including for services in the case studies of Lebak Siliwangi and Tamansari). Key self-organizational traits that shape their nuanced character are summarized.

References

Alzamil A (2018) Evaluating urban status of informal settlements in Indonesia: a comparative analysis of three case studies in North Jakarta. J Sustain Dev 11(4):148–173

Anindito D, Maula F, Akbar R (2018) Modelling the Kampungkota: a quantitative approach in defining Indonesian informal settlements. In: Proceedings of IOP conference series: earth and environmental science

BPS (2022). Accessed from: https://www.bps.go.id/indicator/29/2019/1/proporsi-rumah-tangga-dengan-status-kepemilikan-rumahmilik-dan-sewa-kontrak-menurut-daerah-tempat-tinggal.html

Dovey K, Cook B, Achmadi A (2019) Contested riverscapes in Jakarta: flooding, forced eviction and urban image. Space Polity 23(3):1–19

Firman T (1996) Urbanisasi, Persebaran Penduduk dan Tata Ruang di Indonesia. J PWK (21)

Gultom A (2018) Kalapa—Jacatra—Batavia—Jakarta: an old city that never gets old. J Archaeol Fine Arts Southeast Asia 2(1–27)

Hamidah N, Rijanta R, Setiawan B, Marfai M (2017) "Kampung" as a formal and informal integration model (Case Study: Kampung Pahandut, Central Kalimantan Province, Indonesia). Forum Geogr 31(1):43–55. Accessed from: https://doi.org/10.23917/forgeo.v31i1.3074

Jones P (2017) Formalizing the informal: Understanding the position of informal settlements and slums in sustainable urbanization policies and strategies in Bandung, Indonesia. J Sustain 9(8):1436. Accessed from: https://doi.org/10.3390/su9081436

Jones P (2020) The case for inclusion of international planning studios in contemporary urban planning pedagogy. J Sustain 11(15). Accessed from: http://dx.doi.org/10.3390/su11154174

Kotaku (2020) Tentang program Kota Tanpa Kumuh (Kotaku). Accessed from: http://kotaku.pu.go.id/page/6880/tentang-program-kota-tanpa-kumuh-kotaku

Kusno A (2019) Middling urbanism: the megacity and the Kampung. Urban Geogr 41(7):954–970. Accessed from: https://doi.org/10.1080/02723638.2019.1688535

Leitner H, Sheppard E (2017) From Kampungs to Condos? Contested accumulations through displacement in Jakarta. Environ Plann Econ Space 50(2):437–456

Mardiansjah F, Rahayu P, Rukmana D (2021) New patterns of urbanization in Indonesia: Emergence of non-statutory towns and new extended urban regions. Environ Urban ASIA 12(1):11–26

Milone P (1993) Kampung improvement in the small and medium sized cities of central java. Rev Urban Reg Dev Stud 5(1):74–94

Obermayr C (2017) Sustainable city management: informal settlements in Surakarta, Indonesia. The Urban Book Series, Springer

Pithouse R (2009) A progressive policy without progressive politics: lessons from the failure to implement 'Breaking New Ground'. SSB/TRP/MDM 54. Accessed from: http://abahlali.org/files/01-Pithouse.pdf

Reerink G, van Gelder J (2010) Land titling, perceived tenure security, and housing consolidation in the Kampongs of Bandung, Indonesia. Habitat Int 34(1):78–85

Roberts M, Sander F, Tiwari S (2019) Time to act—Realizing Indonesia's Urban Potential. World Bank Group. Accessed from: file:///C:/Users/prjon/Downloads/9781464813894%20(2).pdf

Rukmana D, Ramadhani D (2021) Income inequality and socioeconomic segregation in Jakarta. Urban Socio-Econ Segregation Income Inequality 135–152. Accessed from: INDONESIA'S URBAN STUDIES (indonesiaurbanstudies.blogspot.com

Rukmana D (2018) Upgrading housing settlement for the urban poor in Indonesia: an analysis of the Kampung Deret program. In: Grant B, Yang Liu C, Ye L (2018) Metropolitan Governance in Asia and the pacific rim: borders, challenges, futures. Springer Nature Singapore. Accessed from: https://doi.org/10.1007/978-981-13-0206-0_5

Setiawan B (2010) Strategi Pengembangan Usaha Kerajinan Bambu di Wilayah Kampung Pajeleran Sukahati Kecamatan Cibinong Kabupaten Bogor. J Manajemen Dan Organisasi 1(2):135–147

Statista (2022) Indonesia: urbanization from 2010 to 2020. Accessed from: https://www.statista.com/statistics/455835/urbanization-in-indonesia/

Suhartini N, Jones P (2019) Urban governance and informal settlements: lessons from the city of Jayapura, Indonesia. The Urban Book Series, Springer Nature, Switzerland

Suhartini S, Jones P (2020) Better understanding self-organizing cities: a typology of order and rules in informal settlements. J Reg City Plann 31(3):237–263. Accessed from: https://doi.org/10.5614/jpwk.2020.31.3.2

Sullivan J (1986) Kampung and state: the role of government in the development of urban community in Yogyakarta. Indonesia 41:63–88

Tunas D, Peresthu A (2010) The self-help housing in Indonesia: the only option for the poor? Habitat Int 34(3):315–322

United National General Assembly (2013) Report of the Special Rapporteur on adequate housing as a component of the right to an adequate standard of living, and on the right to non-discrimination in this context on her mission to Indonesia. Agenda Item 3, Human Rights Council, New York. Accessed from: file:///C:/Users/prjon/Documents/HOME 2020 and 2021/Book and Slum Upgrading/To Read/52e0f5e7a RApportor.pdf

Urbanet (2022) Infograhics: urbanisation and urban development in Indonesia. Accessed from: https://www.urbanet.info/infographics-urbanisation-in-indonesia/

Van der Molen W (1993) Glory of Batavia: the image of a colonial city through the eyes of a Javanese Nobleman, *Urban symbolism*. In: Nas P (ed) Studies in human society series, vol. 8. Brill, Leiden and New York

Voskuil R (1996) Bandoeng, Beeld Van Een Stad (Bandung, Citra Sebuah Kota). Publisher: Purmerend, Asia Maior

Wertheim W (1958) The Indonesian town studies in urban sociology selected studies of Indonesia by Dutch scholars. The Royal Tropical Institute, Amsterdam

Widjaja G (2013) Kampung-kota bandung. Bandung. Graha Ilmu. Accessed from: http://hdl.handle.net/123456789/1572

Wilhelm M (2011) The role of community resilience in adaptation to climate change: The urban poor in Jakarta, Indonesia. In: Otto-Zimmermann K (ed) Resilient cities: cities and adaptation to climate change. Springer, New York

World Bank (2014) Indonesia: A roadmap for housing policy reform. World Bank. Accessed from: databank.worldbank.org

World Bank (2016) Indonesia urban story. Accessed from: https://www.worldbank.org/en/news/feature/2016/06/14/indonesia-urban-story

Chapter 5
Kampung Marlina, Jakarta

Abstract This Chapter analyses the nature of self-organization and how it is expressed in Kampung Marlina as located in North Jakarta, with a major emphasis on understanding patterns of micro-morphology. The context of the kampung's development is assessed, including its small-scale origins in the 1960's and the subsequent path of intensification in the surrounding area by industry. Noting a low proportion of residents having a land certificate, land tenure arrangements plus other socio-economic profiles and the governance role of RTs and RWs are outlined. In terms of morphology, Kampung Marlina is in the form of an irregularly-sized grid with ad-hoc sized blocks linked by alleyways. Linear 'sidewalks' have gradually framed the outer edges of Kampung Marlina, their development paralleling the housing on both sides of the main access street of *Gang Marlina*. Types of access plus density, mix of use, the changing condition of the alleyway/housing interface and typical physical increments added to housing are outlined so as to better understand morphology patterns and adaptation strategies utilized at the local level through self-organization.

Keywords Kampung Marlina · History · Socio-economic · Governance · Morphology

5.1 History of Kampung Marlina

In the 1960s, Muara Baru or Pluit, the urban village where Kampung Marlina is located, was once an area of swamps and ponds. Being part of the larger Penjaringan district of North Jakarta, Muara Baru had minimal residential buildings, estimated by residents to comprise approximately 20 to 25 households at that time. The arable land that was available was used primarily for subsistence farming. By the 1970s, industries and new factories started to be developed in Muara Baru, including paper, textile, cartons, and pen industries. The residents who occupied areas adjacent to the industrial buildings were voluntarily relocated to Kampung Marlina, with residents staking out and claiming lands for their families.

The growth of Muara Baru including Kampung Marlina increased substantially in the early 1980s when a fishing port was built concurrent with the development of new industries and factories. Migrants from outside Jakarta began to arrive and construct

N. Suhartini and P. Jones, *Beyond the Informal*, The Urban Book Series,
https://doi.org/10.1007/978-3-031-22239-9_5

housing in response to the job opportunities created from the activities in the fishing port, industries and warehouses. The basic urban infrastructure built during the period of the Dutch colonialization, including drainage channels, canals, and water reservoirs, increased the land value and attracted the development of housing properties for middle to upper class socio-economic groups. These properties included the Pantai Mutiara resort and Pluit mall, residences and apartments.

With no provision for low-income housing, the urban poor and disadvantaged residents built non-permanent houses and expanded the footprint of Kampung Marlina. The name of Kampung Marlina was taken from the local ballpoint pen factory called "Marlina". In the initial development phase, only people who worked in the local factories resided in Kampung Marlina. However, as workers at the fishing port increased and unemployed residents started building their houses in and adjacent to Kampung Marlina, there grew a heterogenous mix of kampung dwellers. Locations with the lowest supervision and enforcement from the government received the largest intake of residents. Land on the seaside belonged to PT Pelindo, a state-owned company that handling sea-shipping, while other migrants moved onto lands given by the State to private companies to run industrial activities. Residents did not acquire land certificates since the land belonged primarily to either the State or private companies.

The national economic crisis of 1997 saw a major increase in unemployed migrants arriving at Kampung Marlina seeking work and affordable housing. While the national economy improved early in the new millennium, migrants were still attracted to Muara Baru and particularly to Kampung Marlina given the low-skill employment opportunities in the local area. Newcomers built their houses in clusters, often in back lanes and alleyways to be 'out of view' from the main roads to avoid formal inspection and public gaze. Buildings were generally small, on average 18–22 m^2 in area and were box-like in form (Source: interview with RW head). The construction materials used were temporary and recycled, such as cardboard, plastic and iron sheeting. As the financial circumstances of residents improved, residents renovated and improved their housing 'step by step' by adding and extending different rooms for bedrooms, toilets, and storage, often with permanent materials. These renovations and improvements continued in the new millennium as families grew and second and third generation residents had to be accommodated. In 2020, the population density of Kampung Marlina was approximately 32,848 persons per km^2 (Source: interview with RW head).

The younger generations who had employment purchased a house and/or land from de-facto landowners with a payment and receipt called *girik*.[1] The process was simple as it only involved confirmation of the transaction by the head of the RT or a neighbor. The head of the RT or RW then published a notification in the kampung to confirm that the land and/or house has changed ownership (with the land history briefly explained). With a lack of awareness regarding land tenure regulations,

---

[1] Girik is a proof of land ownership made by the owner on customary rights. Girik has been widely used in traditional transactions in many parts of Indonesia and not admitted as a formal proof of land ownership.

residents felt secure on the process of the land title transfer provided there was a witness to the transaction process. It is important to note that local governments do not supervise or register transactions in the informal land market. In Kelurahan Muara Baru (KMB), the informal housing market comprising various forms of payments has been able to meet the rapid demand for shelter. Despite the lack of individual land titles and residential building licenses, the land and housing market remains active and dynamic, filling a major gap caused by a lack of formal housing supply and measures to secure long-term land management. Even though many households do not have a land certificate, KMB residents including those in Kampung Marlina continue to pay land and building taxes to the government.

The number of neighborhood associations (Rukun Tetangga or RT) in KMB has grown extensively, from 12 RTs in the early 1980s to 48 RTs in 2021. The RT representatives are responsible for managing and including the records of the names and origins of the fast-growing undocumented temporary immigrants. They act as informal officers to help with residential arrangements not formally connected with the Kelurahan. For example, within Kampung Marlina, a locality comprising RTs 03 and 05 called Kampung Bengek has been set aside to accommodate migrants with no formal documentation. Most of the residents in Kampung Bengek are those who previously resided in a nearby riverside squatter settlement adjacent to Ciliwung River. They were resettled due to evictions that started in 2013 for river and flood mitigation works which impact wider Jakarta.

The extensive increase in demand for informal housing has occurred because the residents of KMB cannot afford to build and access proper decent housing. When improving their housing, such as undertaking extensions residents inform the RT head, noting they do not have to obtain government permits. This is the accepted protocol and there is no effort to enforce zoning or compliance with planning and building codes. Formal guidance for construction and housing permits do not exist due to lack of education and issues of affordability in meeting these 'high' standards. This has resulted in the production of irregular housing and spatial layouts, often with poor building safety as construction is based merely on the owner's knowledge. The dwellings in the neighborhood are positioned in a ribbon arrangement along the main road or adjoining the nearby Lake Marlina. Homeowners are at risk of both flooding and fire because of poor construction design. The absence of regulations regarding the minimum number of tenants, sanitation standards, maximum density, water supply and drainage have led to poor quality housing. Applicable "local standards" for the latter are agreed via verbal communication and are mediated by the head of the RT.

5.2 Socio-economic Characteristics

Land disputes and the status of buildings have become central issues in Kampung Marlina. As noted, the land which residents occupy belongs primarily to the state and, to a lesser degree, private companies. The national economic crisis of 1997 was a key driver in the State Government allowing unemployed citizens to occupy land and erect housing in the kampung. In consideration of this, it is not surprising that approximately 73.5% of the land ownership in Kampung Marlina is without a land certificate, thus, falling into the category of 'informal tenure' as discussed in Chap. 4. Building usage is primarily household-orientated, with approximately 8.3% of buildings being mixed-use or used for small informal economies. Figure 5.1 presents the building and usage characteristics of Kampung Marlina.

Household to building density at Kampung Marlina is typically one household per dwelling, with the maximum number of households per dwelling being six families. Results of population demographic (2020) surveys show that approximately 210 households comprise 3 to 5 persons, with the number of households consisting of more than 5 persons significantly higher than those comprising 1 to 3 persons. This is further explained by the characteristics of land area size and building floor area. The land area size of the building is varied, starting from 9 to 119 m^2, with average being only 35.6 m^2. With most of the buildings being 2-storeys, the average floor area per building is 71.04 m^2. Thus, each person typically has access to 17.76 m^2 of space within their respective building. In terms of duration of land and building occupation, over 40% of the respondents at Kampung Marlina have resided there between 10 and 27 years. Importantly, 36.25% of residents have occupied their land and buildings within Kampung Marlina between 27 and 40 years as shown in Fig. 5.2.

Residents of Kampung Marlina rely primarily on diverse low-paying jobs to sustain their livelihoods. Household surveys (2021) reveals that most residents (38.67%) work as an employee in the private sector, primarily in the nearby textile factories, or as a local entrepreneur. Approximately 12.15% work as day laborers,

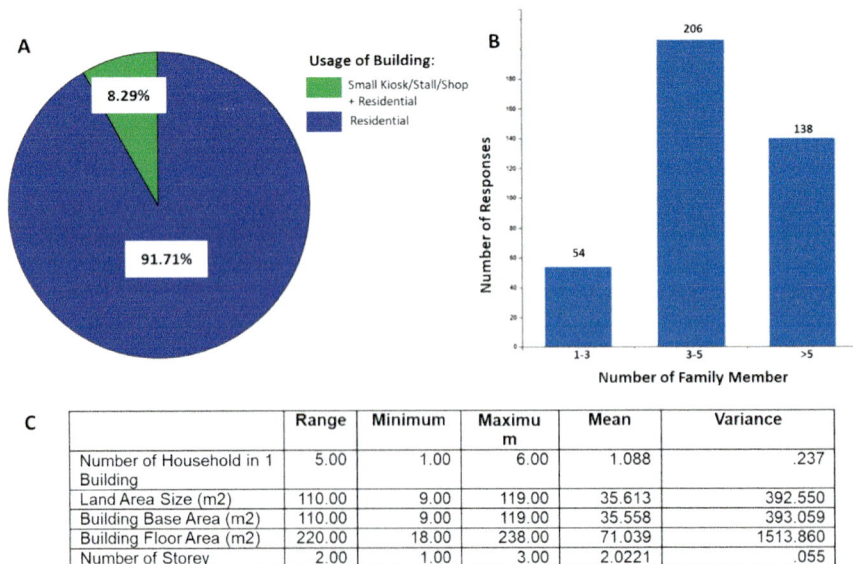

C		Range	Minimum	Maximum	Mean	Variance
	Number of Household in 1 Building	5.00	1.00	6.00	1.088	.237
	Land Area Size (m2)	110.00	9.00	119.00	35.613	392.550
	Building Base Area (m2)	110.00	9.00	119.00	35.558	393.059
	Building Floor Area (m2)	220.00	18.00	238.00	71.039	1513.860
	Number of Storey	2.00	1.00	3.00	2.0221	.055

Fig. 5.1 Settlement characteristics in Kampung Marlina. *Source* Population Demographic Survey (2020)

Fig. 5.2 Types of occupation by resident in Kampung Marlina. *Source* Household Surveys (2021)

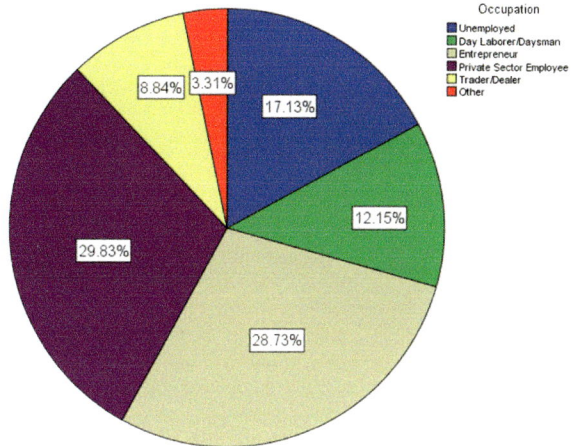

mainly in the fisheries and receive fluctuating low wages. Nearly 9% of residents work as small stall holders attached to their houses or as street hawkers in strategic places, for example, located at entrance ways to schools and at major *gang* (alleyway) intersections. Although most residents are in the productive working age group, approximately 17.13% remain unemployed (Fig. 5.3).

Regarding monthly income, approximately 54% of residents receive below Rp. 1,500,000, with approximately 35% of residents having their monthly income in the Rp 1,500,000 to Rp 3,000,000 range (Household Surveys 2021). This equates to approximately 90% of residents in Kampung Marlina receiving a monthly income well below the Jakarta provincial minimum wage standard of Rp 4,452,724. As such, approximately 35.41% of residents claim to have inadequate monthly incomes to meet their basic household needs (Figs. 5.4 and 5.5).

As shown in the images above, 8.3% of residences in Kampung Marlina comprise diverse small businesses. These are mainly small stalls selling food or small-scale

Fig. 5.3 Street hawkers who adapt to the physical space constraints of changing alleyways alignments are commonplace in Kampung Marlina. *Source* Authors (2019)

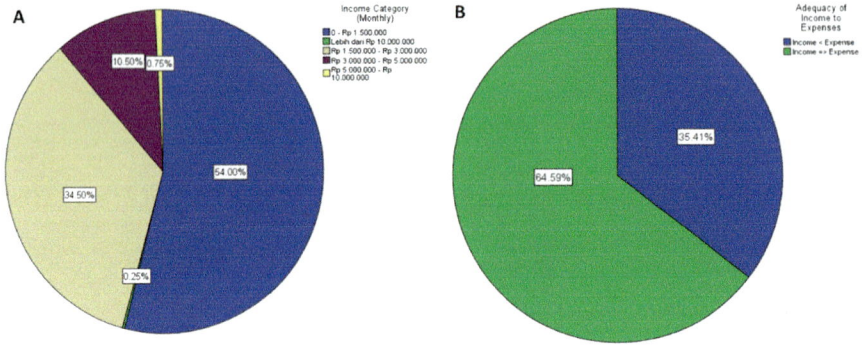

Fig. 5.4 The range of monthly incomes and proportion of income to expenses of Kampung Marlina residents. *Source* Household Surveys (2021)

Fig. 5.5 Typical economic activities in Kampung Marlina are innovative in their use of space. *Source* Household Surveys (2021)

retail goods and are attached to living spaces as part of the entry to residences. Most stalls, whether permanent or temporary, occupy some portion of the alleyway, thus reducing space for the mobility of passing pedestrians and hawkers. The residents of Kampung Marlina fulfill many of their grocery needs from surrounding stalls given the relatively cheaper price of goods purchased locally and available in smaller quantities compared to larger, more distant shopping centers.

5.3 Governance Systems

Urban development in Kampung Marlina, especially for the provision of basic infrastructure, is facilitated by several types of governance. Drainage systems are arranged by formal (that is, the municipal government) and informal governance (as initiated by residents both individually and in groups). Formal government funded drainage systems were built in all RTs except RT 3, RT 10, and RT 11 due to administrative problems over agreed locations related to land issues. The 3 RTs whose drainage system were not built by the government then took initiative to organize their own planning and development of drainage (Figs. 5.6 and 5.7).

For the provision of sanitation, the main mode of governance is through informal provision. Networks of wastewater pipes and drains are maintained by individual households, and to a lesser extent resident groups. Most households in Kampung Marlina use private toilets located inside their dwelling, followed by households using public toilets (MCK) or adjoining private toilets outside of the house. Public toilets are provided by groups and RWs and are used by residents who do not have private toilets as well as by passing pedestrians. The surveys (2021) shows that households using public toilets contribute Rp 2000—Rp 4000 per use cso as to fund leaning fees. Cleaning of septic tanks are arranged informally by individual households and groups (Figs. 5.8, 5.9 and 5.10; Table 5.1).

Stakeholder involvement in Kampung Marlina is reflected in bottom-up and top-down development arrangements. The overarching trend is that the Municipal Government formulates and implements the programs proposed by the RTs and RWs in Kampung Marlina, thus reflecting a co-evolution of stakeholder needs, resources and working together over time. As an urban kampung whose main governance is informal and resident-led, basic mechanisms are employed by stakeholders in

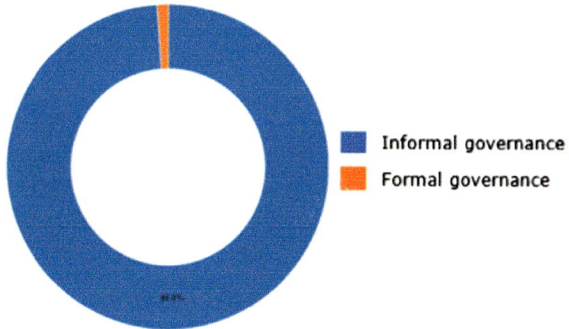

Fig. 5.6 Governance arrangements for the development of drainage. *Source* Household Surveys (2021)

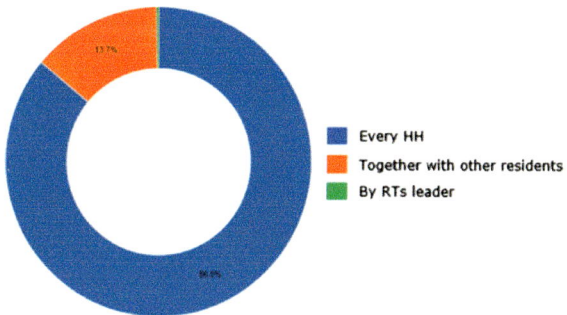

Fig. 5.7 Drainage maintenance systems in Kampung Marlina. *Source* Household Surveys (2021)

Fig. 5.8 The governance of
the existing wastewater
system. *Source* Household
Surveys (2021)

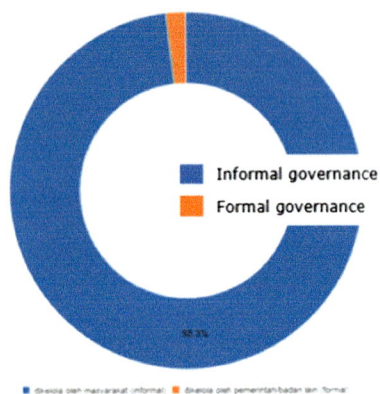

Fig. 5.9 Types of toilet
provision. *Source* Household
Surveys (2021)

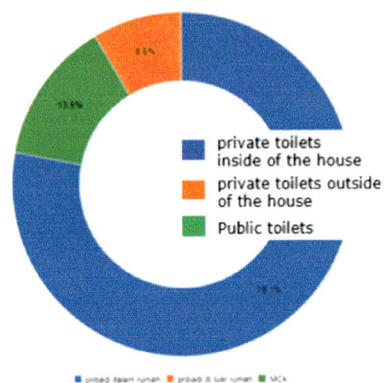

Fig. 5.10 Types of
wastewater pipe network
maintenance. *Source*
Household Surveys (2021)

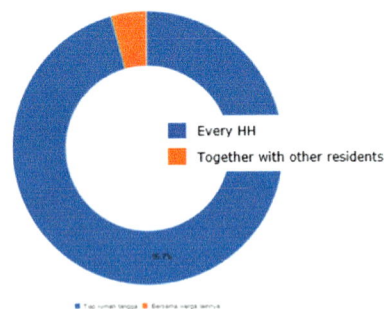

Kampung Marlina in planning basic infrastructure (See Table 5.1). A key leader in
this process is the head of the RT, who plays an integral role in accommodating
residents' aspirations for existing and upgraded infrastructure.

For example, if there are complaints about drainage lines not being cleaned of
debris and causing overflow and local flooding, the head of the RT collates these

Table 5.1 Main modes of infrastructure governance arrangements in Kampung Marlina

Basic urban services	Main modes of governance arrangements		
	Informal	Formal	Hybrid
Drainage	V	V	–
Wastewater system	V	V	–
Toilet	V	–	–
Septic tanks	V	–	-

Source Field Surveys (2021)

concerns and presents them at the development planning meeting *(Musrenbang)* of the North Jakarta Municipal Government. The meeting of the *Musrenbang* is essentially a planning forum of local and state stakeholders who prepare both national and regional development plans. The *Musrenbang* directs the preparation of Government Working Plans or *Rencana Kerja Pemerintah* (RKP) and Regional Government Working Plans or *Rencana Kerja Pemerintah* Daerah (RKPD) which reflects the aspirations of various stakeholders, that is, professional associations, universities, non-governmental organizations, traditional and religious leaders, as well as the business community. Based on the *Musrenbang* deliberations, planning officials will then decide which of the proposed activities are accepted and actioned.

Stakeholders cooperate on identifying priority local needs and collaborate with upper levels of government who have access and varying controls over external funding and its timing. In Kampung Marlina, stakeholders contributing to development plans differ by need, particularly for basic service provision. In the management of drainage systems, for example, local residents, community groups, RT leaders and the Municipal Government are all actively involved in providing this service. The Municipal Government contributes by maintaining bitumen *gangs* and roads in all RTs (except RT 3, 10, and 11), which includes providing formal drainage on both road verges. The 3 RTs whose drainage systems were not managed by the Municipal Government initiated the building and governance over their own drainage. The stakeholders involved in wastewater facilities are residents, regional officials (RTs leaders up to the District head; see Fig. 5.13), community groups, womens association and youth associations, Municipal Government and the private sector. An example of this can be seen with the private company Pelindo which provides land for public toilets in Kampung Marlina (Figs. 5.11 and 5.12).

Submission of local needs by residents and local groups are received by the RT leader on an annual basis. In addition to the availability of funds, the realization of the plans as submitted to and agreed by the *Musrenbang* depends on the level and prioritization of need and the urgency of the activities. In Kampung Marlina, the realization process for larger infrastructure activities such as water supply upgrades takes between one to three years after the activity is endorsed by the *Musrenbang* and the necessary funding allocated. Parallel to the work of the *Musrenbang* are the voluntary works carried out by the residents for maintaining basic infrastructure, such as drain forming, cleaning and rubbish removal when public bins overflow. An

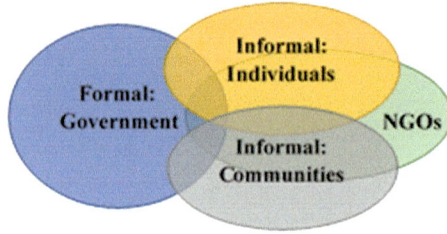

Fig. 5.11 The range of stakeholders contributing to development in Kampung Marlina. *Source* Authors

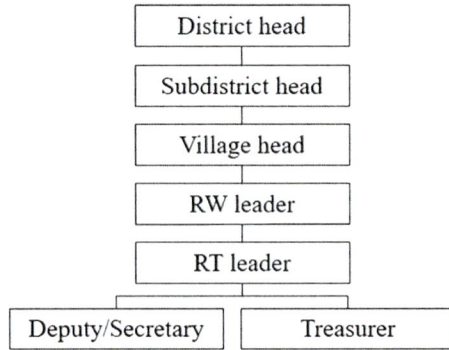

Fig. 5.12 Formal stakeholders involved in the development of Kampung Marlina. *Source* Authors

Fig. 5.13 Kampung Marlina in the Penjaringan District, adjacent to Sunda Kelapa Seaport and the industrial/warehouse area. *Source* Authors (2022)

example is the development of drainage systems in RTs 3, 10 and 11 which were not covered by government funding. In these instances, NGOs such as the Rujak Center offer technical assistance to build communal toilet facilities. However, these offers are sometimes rejected by residents due to contention over the 'correct' location, the acquisition of land and funding, plus the responsibility for ongoing maintenance of the facilities.

5.4 Morphological Evolution

Dovey and King (2011) identified the predominant morphological types characterizing informal settlements and their formation in the formal city in South and Southeast Asian cities. The key types identified were urban waterfronts, escarpments, and the interstitial easements framing transport infrastructure and other backstage spaces behind the formal street facade. Using this typology developed by Dovey and King (2011) to better understand the varying array of spatial patterns of informal settlements, Kampung Marlina can be organized into three basic morphology types: district, sidewalk and backstage. Kampung Marlina is a 'district' type of informal settlement because its development is inseparable from the history of the Penjaringan district. As noted previously, Kampung Marlina is amongst the oldest informal settlement in the Penjaringan district which emerged in 1960s and 1970s when new factories were being developed in the local area. The locality was considered unattractive for housing as it comprised swampy low-lying lands which were far from Jakarta's city center. The major industry of the area was Kampung Marlina's ballpoint factory, which was a magnet attracting migrants seeking employment and provided an opportunity to secure affordable land near their workplace. In the 1980s, the district expanded through the development of the Sunda Kelapa Port. This expansion offered further employment opportunities in cargo transportation, primarily the loading and unloading of metals, timber and other household goods to and from other islands in Indonesia. All these developments contributed to the mixed-use 'district' type" as it now exists in Kampung Marlina which comprises housing, industrial, and transportation functions (Fig. 5.13).

Kampung Marlina reflects an irregular-sized grid comprising ad-hoc sized blocks linked by alleyways. Linear 'sidewalks' have gradually framed the outer edges of Kampung Marlina, their development paralleling the housing on both sides of the main access street of *Gang Marlina*. Based on interviews with local residents who have occupied Kampung Marlina since the early 1970s, the *gang* was built approximately 3.5 m in width to accommodate trucks accessing the original warehouse buildings. These lands currently stand empty, being designated for future office buildings. The main access road of *Gang Marlina* was developed between the industrial blocks to serve all the warehouses. *Gang Marlina* was initially free from any buildings on both sides of the road reserve so as to provide clear access and traffic throughfare. However, over time and with the increase in migrants and subsequent demands for services of the ever-growing Kampung Marlina, the setback of approximately

Fig. 5.14 Sidewalk housing characterizing Kampung Marlina. *Source* Authors (2021)

5 m from the edge of the street to the land boundary and building line has been encroached. Most of the residents who reside here are low-skilled workers employed in the warehouses who self-organize their housing using a mix of materials. However, some of the publicly visible housing comprising the sidewalk and perimeter frontage blocks whose setbacks have been reduced are constructed with permanent materials (Fig. 5.14).

Kampung Marlina can also be viewed as a 'backstage' type of informal settlement. In 1990s, the land was considered abandoned and leftover land which families could occupy at will. Housing was 'inserted' behind large industrial areas where the settlement would not be visible from the main road known as Jalan Muara Baru. There is only one entry point to Kampung Marlina that can be accessed by car, with the other entries to *gangs* being relatively narrow and no more than 1.5 m in width. These *gangs* are for pedestrians and bike use only.

In 2020, Kampung Marlina was identified as a priority informal settlement for upgrading by the Jakarta Province based on a set of upgrading criteria. One key criterion was population density given overcrowding and high population densities strongly characterize Kampung Marlina. With limited land area, residents in the new millennium have developed their houses vertically with building heights now ranging up to six storeys. Based on interviews with local leaders and results of Household Surveys, the gross coverage of built area to plot size equates to approximately

97%. There is no green space available in Kampung Marlina; the only unbuilt space being the network of alleyways.

Deconstructing types of access plus density, mix of use, and the changing condition of the alleyway/housing interface can be used to better understand and interpret morphology patterns at the local level (Kamalipour 2016a). There are three main access points at Kampung Marlina (see Fig. 5.15). The first access point is via *Jalan* Karta Jaya at Kampung Kembangan Lestari (with the southern side connecting to the Pluit Residential Apartment complex). The second point is via the main entrance of *Jalan* Marlina. The third point is connected through Kampung Elektro which directly adjoins Kampung Marlina from the northern side. This *Jalan* is the only 'public space' used by children and youth across the entire Kampung Marlina.

As the main access entrance, *Jalan* Marlina divides the Kampung into two major areas to the north and south. It also is the only *Jalan* accessible by cars and trucks and thus provide access to the inner warehousing area adjacent to the sea, as located across from the Sunda Kelapa seaport. A narrow *gang* with a varying width of 2–3 m extends approximately 397 m and connects both sides of Kampung Marlina from Kampung Kembangan Lestari to Kampung Elektro. With an average block size of 15–60 square meters and with minimal 'dead end' minor alleyways, Kampung Marlina is well-connected by a network of traversable alleyways. Within the southern side (RT 01, 02, 08, and 09), connectivity is relatively good to excellent, while the rest of RTs in the northern part having some 'cul-de-sac' alleyways especially in the west side of the kampung.

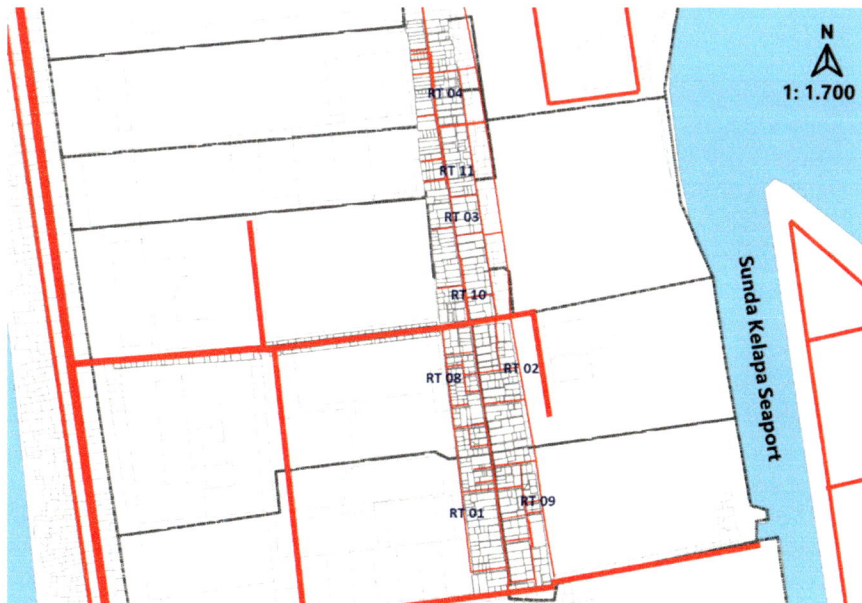

Fig. 5.15 Access network at Kampung Marlina. *Source* Authors

The functional mix of Kampung Marlina is primarily residential, interspersed with a small number of community facilities such as schools, mosques, modest healthcare facilities plus home-based permanent, temporary and mobile businesses. Hyper-functionality as seen in Kampung Marlina is a system in which residents connect a shop/stall or *warung* to their private spaces as a land use extension, or construct a shop/stall/*warung* wholly on the ground floor with their living spaces on the upper floors. This flexibility of spaces to facilitate varying functions allows for a direct connection between the public and private areas at the ground floor level. For example, stairs fronting alleyways are used to hang clothes and toys for sale. Multi-functionality is also seen in the temporality of spaces which have different uses at varying times of the day, such as a window used for ventilation and public gaze during the evenings being transformed into a retail shop front during the day. Mini-stores that are expressed in multiple physical and spatial configurations are popular. These tend to be concentrated along the main north–south alleyways where there are higher concentrations of foot traffic than in other parts of the kampung. The alleyway system based on an irregular grid layout offers a higher level of street activity for children playing, as well as facilitating sociality and a hierarchy of functional hyperactivity (Fig. 5.16).

By using the interface typology parameters as developed by Dovey and Wood (2015) and Jones (2021a, b), three primary types of public gaze and visibility can be identified in Kampung Marlina. These include direct/transparent, direct/opaque, and impermeable/blank, notwithstanding they can also occur in combinations. The direct/transparent interface facilitates viewing in and out of the dwelling. This includes maintaining a public gaze through attached shops on the ground floor of the residential building. This type usually consists of an entrance and a transparent shop front or opening that may be utilized for exchanging products and making purchases without having to enter the store (Kamalipour 2016b). If the shop is connected to other rooms on the ground level, it also provides a direct visual link into and out of the private space into the alleyway.

The second form of gaze which is the most common in Kampung Marlina is direct/opaque walls. Homes with an opaque ground floor entrance have a direct access way but the visibility into and out of the public and private spaces is restricted by an opaque fence or partial wall. There is little social or commercial interaction at the entryway of this visual interface (Kamalipour 2016a). To gain entry to residences, family members enter a semi-private zone before proceeding to internal private spaces.

The third form of public gaze and accessway is impermeable/blank walls, where no access or gaze is allowed. This is most common in corner residences where access (with or without windows) defines the side boundary fronting a minor alleyway.

Both the direct/transparent and direct/opaque gaze and access typologies may contain a setback (Jones 2021b). This intermediatory space retreats from the legal and or physical boundary behind the alleyway alignment, with or without a fence, and with an opaque or direct/indirect view. Residents in Kampung Marlina utilize these spaces for seating, motorcycle parking, drying clothes, socializing and both permanent and temporary mini-stores (Fig. 5.17).

Fig. 5.16 A functional mix of buildings characterizes Kampung Marlina. *Source* Authors (2021)

5.5 Strategies of Adaptation

Adaptation strategies in Kampung Marlina have been identified using the frameworks and analytical tools used to understand micro-physical changes as developed by Dovey and Wood (2015), Jones (2021a) and Kamalipour (2016a). The most common physical adaptation undertaken by residents in Kampung Marlina are room and floor additions. As evidenced in the socio-economic characteristics of the kampung, most dwellers are employed in the informal economic sector with uncertain and low wages. Approximately 90% of residents earn a monthly family income below the provincial

IMPERMEABLE/BLANK   DIRECT/OPAQUE   DIRECT/TRANSPARENT

SETBACK

Fig. 5.17 Examples of the primary types of public gaze and visibility existing in Kampung Marlina. *Source* Authors (2021)

minimum wage, indicating they live well below the poverty level. However, approximately 65% of residents have lived in the kampung for more than one generation, with many households experiencing the addition of new family members. To fulfil their housing needs and demand for extra space, residents add new rooms incrementally after they have collected sufficient income for the room additions. Increasingly, many residents add more bedrooms for renting purposes. Rental rooms are typically built on the upper floor with stairs constructed in the dwelling setback, thus limiting light, ventilation and gaze to the private spaces at the ground floor. This push to renew and add rooms to dwellings is driven by the fact residents are aware of the strategic location of Kampung Marlina for job opportunities in the adjoining fish market, warehousing and port activities.

Due to the small plot sizes and existing built coverage, room additions in Kampung Marlina have usually occurred vertically in upper floors. Some housing, particularly those situated along the *Jalan Marlina* (the main access), started only in the form

Fig. 5.18 Examples of multiple room additions made to housing. *Source* Authors (2021)

of 'box-houses'. As residents collected sufficient resources and/or their family size increased, upper floors were constructed. At the ground level, changes are mixed; most households maximize their side and front setbacks to increase rooms sizes or add a toilet. The latter can be directly connected to the sewerage and drainage network. With minimal or no development regulation and building changes being resident and household-led, some parts of the drainage system become buried or covered in the process of providing extra spaces for room additions (Fig. 5.18).

Another common type of adaptation at Kampung Marlina is materiality replacement. Many houses in Kampung Marlina were constructed with very limited resources, using cheap, recycled, and temporary materials to develop their housing and secure their plot. Following a gradual improvement in household economic stability, dwellers improve building construction quality or replace damaged and deteriorated materials, such as roofing materials, often for safety reasons. Residents indicated that tile roofing is also replaced by corrugated iron sheeting as it allows for rainwater collection. This form of adaptation might also be undertaken when dwellers add or extend a new room, thus changing to more permanent and robust materials. This includes materials being replaced from wood and plywood to brick and block materials. While it is more common to switch construction materials as part of undertaking larger increments such as a room, it can also be done as a standalone change. It is space-neutral to replace an old existing material with a new one or move from temporary materials to more permanent ones (Kamalipour 2016a) (Fig. 5.19).

Another type of adaptation observed in Kampung Marlina incorporates a mix of functions, particularly those of residential and retail purposes carried out in external spaces adjoining and abutting the alleyways. With built form changes, these functional activities whether permanent or temporary contribute to the irregular alignment of the alleyway. Many building extensions in Kampung Marlina take the form of second and third floor verandas or balconies, which provides space for surveillance, ventilation and fulfilment of daily chores. As local development or building codes are non-existent or minimal, some dwellers develop balconies in excess of more than 50% of the laneway width below. In terms of internal spaces, residents divide the existing internal space to modify or accommodate new functions such as a ground level stall/mini-shop/*warung*. As noted above, these adaptations are primarily

Fig. 5.19 Extension adaptations undertaken by households in Kampung Marlina. *Source* Authors (2021)

concentrated along the north–south laneways as the intensity of mobility and levels of street-life, economic exchange and sociality are much higher compared to the east–west alleyways of Kampung Marlina (Fig. 5.20).

In terms of public/private interface changes, three types of adaptation can be observed in the development of housing intensification at Kampung Marlina (Jones 2021b). These interface types can occur in multiple configurations. The first is an adaptation to the setback, which is the private and semi-private space in front of dwellings that is modified through adding extra built space, reducing the setback and/or changing fencing to reduce public gaze and increase privacy and security. The second interface change is removing the setback through built form infill, thus aligning the dwelling with the property boundary or building line which defines the

SETBACK ADAPTATION   DIRECT TRANSPARENT TO   IMPERMEABLE TO DIRECT TRANSPARENT
                          SETBACK/PEDESTRIAN

Fig. 5.20 Connon interface adaptations in Kampung Marlina. *Source* Authors (2021)

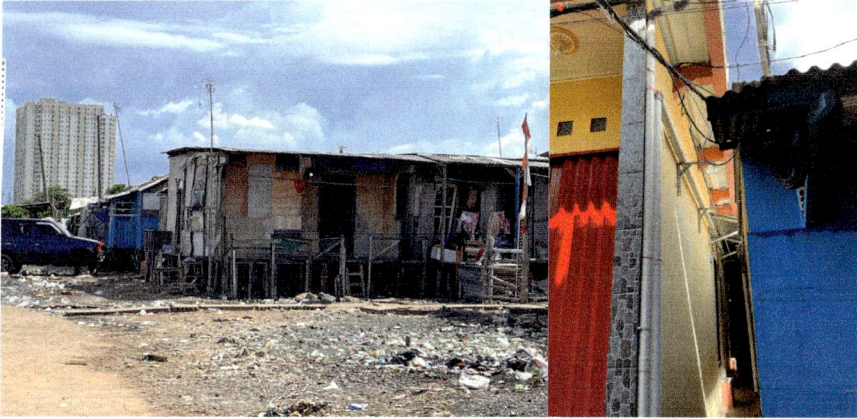

Fig. 5.21 Fluid and flexible property and built boundaries are a commonly accepted practice in the incremental housing process in Kampung Marlina. *Source* Authors (2021)

alleyway alignment. The third interface adaptation is the set-forward, where the form and/or function additions to the dwelling move the boundaries of the property and/or building line forward into the alleyway. As seen in the other case studies, this type of interface adaptation is increasingly common and can occur in conjunction with a setback reduction or full alignment change to where the setback of the dwelling no longer exists (Fig. 5.21).

5.6   Conclusion

The case study of Kampung Marlina reflects the evolution of a range of adaptation measures anchored in informal arrangements which have emerged in the absence of formal and normative governance. These socio-physical 'bottom-up' adaptation initiatives which occur in a non-linear fashion strongly underpin the processes of self-organization. The kampung's housing development and the sustaining of livelihoods is strongly tied to the development of the area for warehousing, fisheries and port development. Self-organized arrangements for governance have emerged to fill the gap so as to enable land, housing and infrastructure provision. Multiple residents and households undertaking their own self-organized building changes on fluid land tenure and flexible building lines results in many unexpected outcomes, such as diverse housing designs and built density, materiality, alleyway encroachment and mixed uses.

The presence of self-organized governance arrangements as strongly tied to the existence of RTs and RWs provide a sense of local security whilst maintaining a level of social amenity that residents, including migrants, tolerate and find acceptable. While these arrangements have not been fully acknowledged by formal governance as part of their development and management structures, the RT and RW leaders have the support of residents to access on their behalf different service provisions, local and formal resources, and to communicate with governments. The election of RT and RW leaders provides some form of local accountability and responsibility to secure basic kampung needs. Importantly, the ongoing tenure of RT and RW leaders as elected by residents as 'one of their own' legitimizes the myriad self-organization activities of residents as reflected in their implied and explicit rules, regulations and protocols.

The evolution of Kampung Marlina shows how locally self-organized communal structures gradually received formal recognition as important stakeholders in managing local urban development activities. Community representatives as seen in RT and RW leaders have expanded their role from community facilitators deliberating on local development issues and land management conflicts, to being part of the city's formal systems seeking higher-level clarity on the legal status of land and infrastructure provision via municipal development plans. In the context of urban planning, the self-organized structures at the local community level in Kampung Marlina and their identification of needs are increasingly connected to the macro-city level plans. RT and RW leaders add in local details and deconstruct kampung complexity in the hope that larger scale spatial and development plans can be more efficient and effective in meeting needs if they are prioritized and resourced. Embracing self-organized arrangements and activities over time strongly tied to local adaptation measures will potentially empower residents as legitimate beneficiaries and stakeholders in the higher-level urban planning and development processes. This will also address the gap faced by the government in terms of finite resource availability as self-organized structures, as demonstrated in Kampung Marlina, can contribute in supporting the provision of land, skills, community capital and other resources 'on the ground' more economically and quickly.

In conclusion, the case study reflects how Kampung Marlina fills the void in accommodating affordable housing and meeting the needs of varying housing sub-markets (renters, owners, sharers, etc.). The kampung also challenges the 'one size fits all' development perspective applied by formal governance mechanisms in terms of infrastructure provision. The kampung acts as a hub and refuge by providing links to informal (and formal) jobs, affordable housing, retail, religious and health needs and service networks. The incremental housing process by self-organization effectively represents the individual expression and endeavors by each family unit. Self-organized governance as developed in Kampung Marlina shows the ability to sustain new and changing demands for increasing services as population density increases, whilst adapting to meeting local household needs as expressed in multiple built form adaptations, configurations and alleyway encroachments over time. Mutual understanding and tolerance are the key ideological traits practiced by most leaders and residents in Kampung Marlina. This framework makes resolving local challenges ranging from neighborly disputes to infrastructure and service provision more amenable. This is because residents and groups are willing to set aside differences regarding decisions which relate to kampung-wide interests.

References

Dovey K, King R (2011) Forms of informality: morphology and visibility of informal settlements. Built Environ 37(1):11–29. Accessed from: https://doi.org/10.2148/benv.37.1.11

Dovey K, Wood S (2015) Public/private urban interfaces: type, adaptation, assemblage. J Urbanism Int Res Placemaking Urban Sustain 8(1):1–16. Accessed from: https://doi.org/10.1080/17549175.2014.891151

Jones P (2021a) The role of adaptation in changing the micro-morphology of informal settlements. In: Raimo D, Lehmann S, Melis A (eds) Earthscan informality through sustainability. pp 180–195

Jones P (2021b) Distance and proximity matters: understanding housing transformation through micro-morphology in informal settlements. Int J Housing Pract Spec Ed Informal Hous Pract 21(2):1–27. Accessed from: https://doi.org/10.1080/19491247.2020.1818052

Kamalipour H (2016a) Forms of informality and adaptations in informal settlements. Int J Architectural Res Archnet-IJAR 10(3):60–75. Accessed from: https://doi.org/10.26687/archnet-ijar.v10i3.1094

Kamalipour H (2016b) Urban morphologies in informal settlements: a case study. Contour J 1(2). Accessed from: https://doi.org/10.6666/contour.v1i2.61

Chapter 6
Kampung Pakualaman, Yogyakarta

Abstract This Chapter analyses the nature of self-organization and how it is expressed in Kampung Pakualaman, Yogyakarta, with a major emphasis on understanding patterns of micro-morphology. The context of the kampung development is assessed, including its history and composition based on four smaller villages, namely, Kampung Jagalan (RW 1), Kampung Beji (RW 2 and 3), Kampung Purwokinanti (RW 4–6), and Kampung Kepatihan (RW 7–10). In terms of land tenure, many residents indicated they had obtained legal land status by acquiring land certificates, noting that more than 80% of household respondents had lived in their dwellings for more than 15 years. More than half of households indicated they receive an income of less than Rp 1,500,000 per month which is below the 2021 Central Java provincial minimum wage of Rp 1,798,979. The provision of basic urban services in Kampung Pakualaman is delivered by different types of governance arrangements, namely, hybrid, formal and informal governance. Increments of morphology include various sidewalk types that have developed alongside housing in Kampung Pakualaman, including sidewalks fronting the Code River. Many inner sections of Kampung Pakualaman known as 'backstages' represent a labyrinth of narrow alleyways where multiple physical adaptation measures connect lower quality and older housing. The key features of self-organization in Kampung Pakualaman are summarized.

Keywords Kampung Pakualaman · History · Socio-economic · Governance · Morphology

6.1 History of Kampung Development

Kadipaten Pakualaman is one of the four original kingdoms of Java (Praja Kejawen) which extended over the entire island of Java and partly onto the island of Borneo in Kerajaan Mataram Islam. On September 23rd, 1754, the political agreement known as the Giyanti Agreement was arranged between the Mataram Kingdom (represented by Prince Mangkubumi) and the Dutch. The Giyanti Agreement saw half of Kerajaan Mataram ceded to Dutch control. In 1755, the remaining Kerajaan Mataram area was divided into the two regions of Surakarta and Yogyakarta. Both of these regions were further split into two, with Yogyakarta being divided into Kasultanan Yogyakarta and Pakualaman.

Pakualaman was created as a princely state in 1812 as a reward for Natakusuma (later named Duke Paku Alam I) for supporting the British in suppressing civil unrest in the then Sultanate of Yogyakarta (Wikipedia 2022). The system of government in Pakualaman is similar to the system in Keraton (traditional Javanese kingdom) given Pakualaman emerged from parts of Kasultanan where the rulers had strong kin ties to the relatives of Keraton (Interview with local resident 2021). The Pakualaman area crosses over both the inside and outside of the city of Yogyakarta, as seen in the area of Kulon Progo. There are special areas for the Keraton in Yogyakarta, including the Pakualaman Ground and the Sultan Ground. One of the privileges of the Pakualaman area is that it was not contained in customary land rules because some of the land was considered to belong to the Pakualaman noblemen (Interview with resident 2021).

Over time, remnants of government systems that existed before independence have been maintained. This includes the socio-political categories of 'resident', 'village', 'Kemantren' (in the city) and 'Kapanewon' (outside the city). The term 'kelurahan', for example, is relatively new and gained popularity in the 1970s, though it was originally used in some contexts to mean 'kampung'.

Kampung Pakualaman consists of four smaller villages: Kampung Jagalan (RW 1), Kampung Beji (RW 2 and 3), Kampung Purwokinanti (RW 4–6), and Kampung Kepatihan (RW 7–10). The overarching Kampung leaders have an office term of five years and are elected by laws applying to the electoral system. The elected leaders of the RWs and RTs leaders serve only three years. The Kampung leaders oversee development affairs and the RW and RT leaders manage the day-to-day administrative matters. One of the unique features of Kampung Pakualaman is that communication from RT and RW leaders to the Kampung leader is made directly by family members as opposed to bureaucratic processes. The RT and RW leaders act as formal government representatives in accommodating resident needs and mediating disputes for basic urban services and land maters for consideration by Kampung leaders and the Municipal Government. The presence of formally-appointed leaders dealing with local issues in RTs and RWs in informal settlements assists in maintaining a form of 'governance equilibrium' (Suhartini and Jones 2019).

6.2 Socio-economic Characteristics

Like other kampungs, the evolution of Kampung Pakualaman reflects a unique development history. In terms of land tenure, most respondents interviewed indicated they had obtained legal land status by acquiring land certificates, followed by residents who had informal agreements for usage and building rights as shown in Fig. 6.1.

Regarding land and building occupation, household surveys (2021) shows that more than 80% of household respondents had lived in their premises for more than 15 years. Approximately 7.5% of respondents in Kampung Pakualaman have

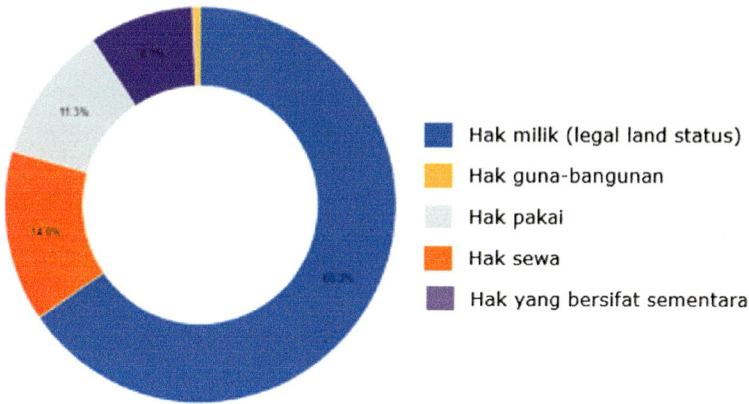

Fig. 6.1 Status of land ownership in Kampung Pakualaman. *Source* Household Surveys (2021)

been living there for 10–15 years, while some 4.4% of respondents had been living there for 5–10 years and for less than 5 years as shown in Fig. 6.2.

Furthermore, household surveys (2021) finds that the number of family members per household in Kampung Pakualaman is skewed towards smaller households, with 76% of households having less than 5 residents, while 24% of households having greater than 5 residents (Fig. 6.3). This is one indicator of population density in Kampung Pakualaman.

In terms of the range of incomes, more than half of households indicated they receive less than Rp 1,500,000 per month. This is below the 2021 Central Java provincial minimum wage of Rp 1,798,979. The second largest group of respondents reported a monthly salary between Rp 1,500,000—Rp 3,000,000 (28%), followed by 10.7% of respondents who received a monthly salary between Rp 3,000,000—Rp 5,000,000. Only 2.7% of households had a monthly salary between Rp 5,000,000—Rp 10,000,000 (Fig. 6.4).

Fig. 6.2 Length of household occupation in Kampung Pakualaman. *Source* Household Surveys (2021)

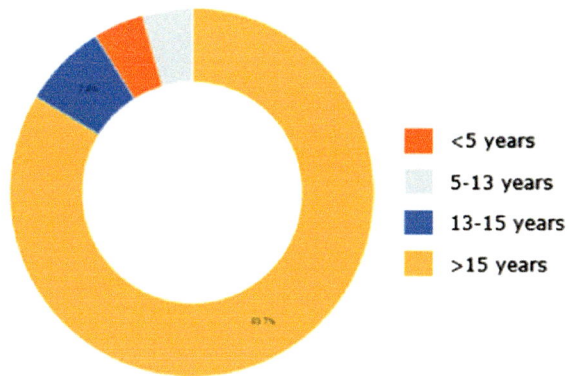

Fig. 6.3 Reported
household size in Kampung
Pakualaman. *Source*
Household Surveys (2021)

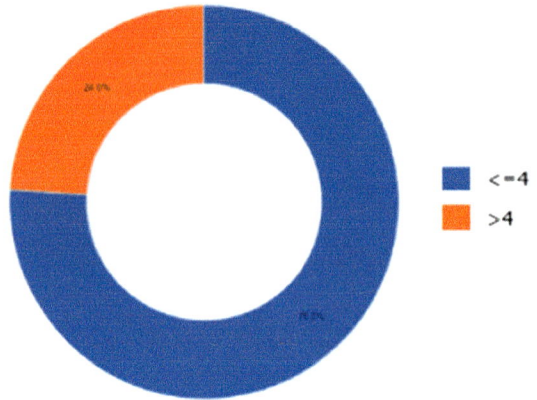

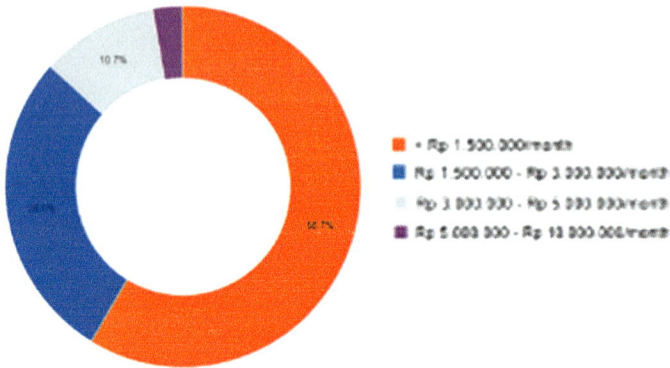

Fig. 6.4 The range of monthly income of household residents in Kampung Pakualaman. *Source* Household Surveys (2021)

The occupations of residents are reported in Fig. 6.5. The most popular occupation accounted for approximately 32.67% of respondents who worked as an entrepreneur, followed by housewife (27.33%). Private sector employees comprised 18.67% of the resident population, as well as other (13.33%), student (6%), labourer/worker (4.67%), unemployed (4.67%), government employees (2.67%), and army/police officer (2%).

6.3 Governance Systems

The provision of basic urban services in Kampung Pakualaman are delivered by different types of governance arrangements. Drainage in Kampung Pakualaman is

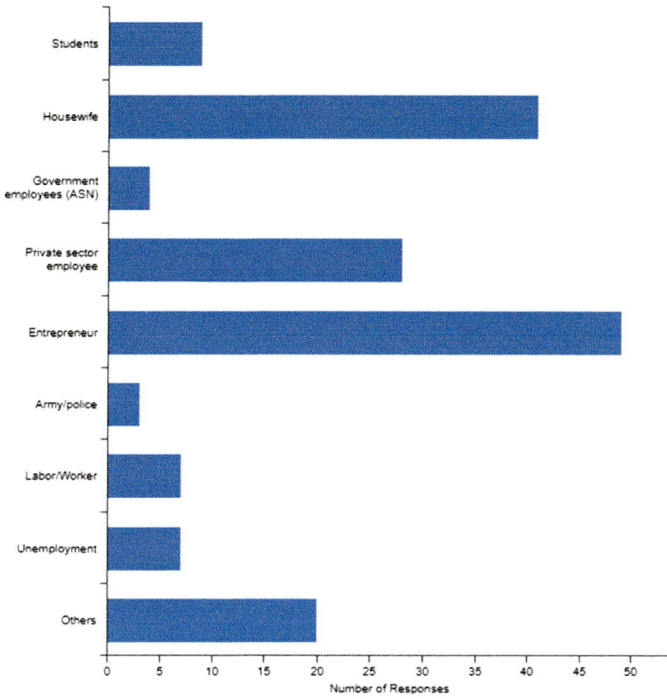

Fig. 6.5 The occupations of residents in Kampung Pakualaman. *Source* Household Surveys (2021)

Fig. 6.6 Governance arrangement of the development of drainage systems. *Source* Household Surveys (2021)

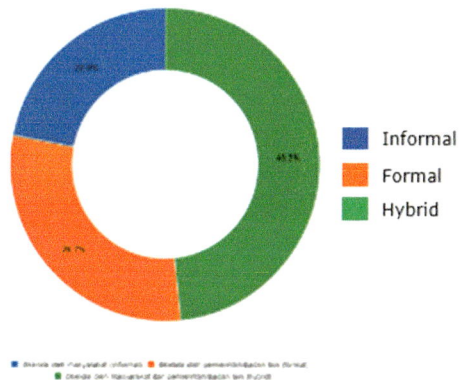

provided by hybrid (that is, residents and government), formal (the municipal government), and informal governance (residents both individually and in groups). This can be seen in Fig. 6.6. The drainage system in Kampung Pakualaman was initially built in the colonial era with open and underground pipe systems. Most houses have a wastewater pipe network connected to an external drain maintained by households and managed by RT leaders. According to the Spatial Plan of Yogyakarta City (RTRW

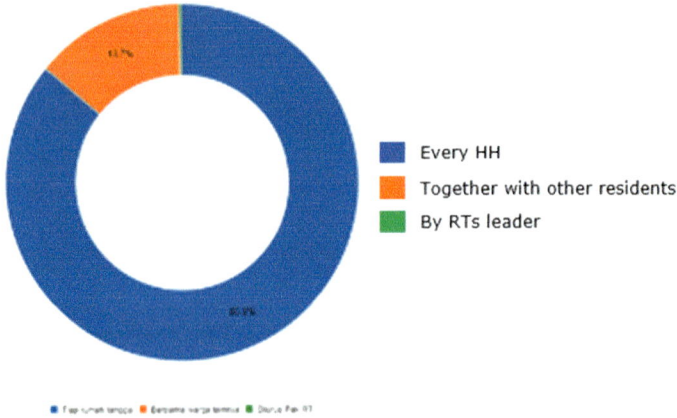

Fig. 6.7 Drainage maintenance systems. *Source* Household Surveys (2021)

Kota Yogyakarta 2021–2041), a drainage system refers to a system developed by combining conventional drainage and applying the concept of green infrastructure to maintain and improve the function of water absorption. The aim is to achieve zero run-off; that is, a condition where the amount of runoff water that is expelled by the drainage system reaches or is close to zero (Fig. 6.7).

In terms of sanitation provision in Kampung Pakualaman, the main mode of governance arrangements is informal. Most households reported using internal private toilets, followed by private toilets external to the house, and additionally there are three public toilet facilities (MCK). Public toilets are built on individual land plots where the land has been donated by the owner. These are used by residents who do not have private toilets, noting kampung men perform evening RT and RW security patrols being members of the 'night watch' as organized through local governance. Septic tanks are also arranged by informal governance. Most of the households have access to one tank which is connected to a communal septic tank external to the house. See Table 6.1 for the complete summary (plus Figs. 6.8, 6.9 and 6.10).

Basic urban services	Main modes of governance arrangements		
	Informal	Formal	Hybrid
Drainage	V	V	V
Wastewater system	V	V	V
Toilet	V	–	–
Septic tanks	V	–	–

Table 6.1 The main modes of governance arrangements for the provision of basic urban services in Kampung Pakualaman

Source Household Surveys (2021)

Fig. 6.8 The governance of the wastewater systems. *Source* Household Surveys (2021)

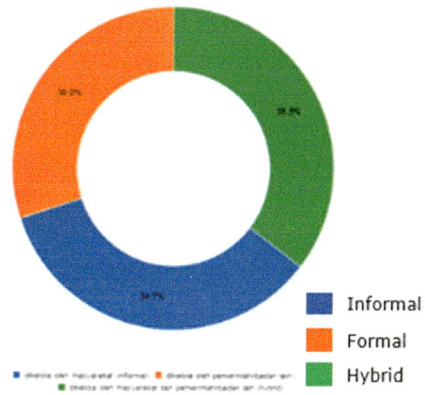

Fig. 6.9 Toilet provision. *Source* Household Surveys (2021)

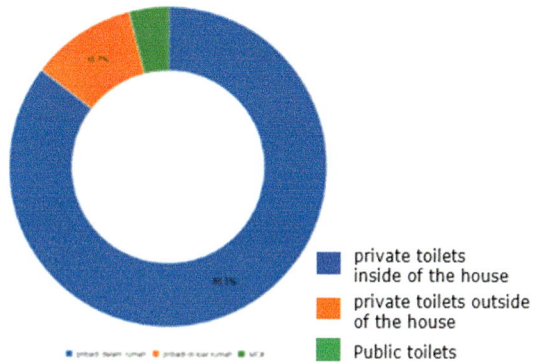

Fig. 6.10 Maintenance responsibility of wastewater pipe networks. *Source* Household Surveys (2021)

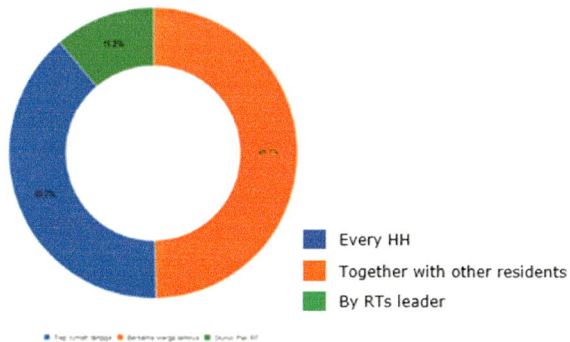

In terms of stakeholder involvement at Kampung Pakualaman, there are various stakeholders involved in development planning arrangements. For drainage, residents, community groups and the Municipal Government (Fig. 6.11) complete the physical works. Similarly, the stakeholders involved in wastewater management consists of residents, local and regional officials (RT leaders and the District head),

Fig. 6.11 The stakeholders contributing to the development and physical provision of basic services in Kampung Pakualaman. *Source* Interviews with Stakeholders (2021)

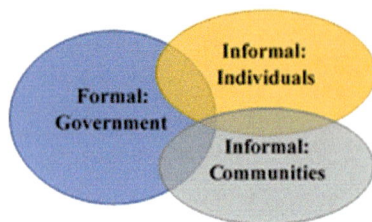

Fig. 6.12 The formal stakeholders involved the provision of basic services in Kampung Pakualaman. *Source* Interviews with Stakeholders (2021)

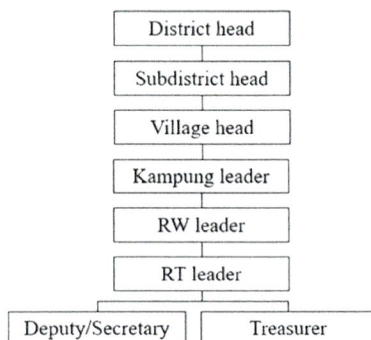

community groups and the Municipal Government. The Municipal Government is the key stakeholder who coordinates and realizes the local programs proposed by the RTs, RWs, and Kampung Leaders in Kampung Pakualaman. KORAMIL (the Indonesian Army territorial units located at the sub-district level) have also assisted in providing public toilets, especially along the riverbank (Fig. 6.12).

Kampung Pakualaman has its own method of undertaking basic infrastructure planning. For program/project submissions to be considered in the *Musrenbang,* the main areas proposed are physical works, i.e., road, alleyway, toilet and sewerage works. In addition to submitting program proposals through the *Musrenbang,* RW heads in Pakualaman Village also submit program and project proposals through the PNPM Mandiri. This nationally-funded scheme provides funding assistance that is primarily targeted at housing, roads, sanitation and water connections at the village level. One of the projects that has been approved and realized with financial assistance in Kampung Pakualaman is a minor road upgrade paralleling an RW boundary.

6.4 Morphological Evolution

Kampung Pakualaman has developed since the Mataram Islam Kingdom was divided into two regions in 1755 and further divided again into 2 localities, one of which was to become Kampung Pakualaman. Over time, Kampung Pakualaman has grown to be a mixed-use district. Approximately 75% of the kampung area is allocated for residential use and building coverage of plots accounts for approximately 80%. Approximately 20% of the area is allocated for high density residential and commercial development. The commercial areas are developed along the outer kampung edges, while housing comprises the inner portions of the kampung alongside the Code River. Some of the area has been zoned for tourism and cultural-educational heritage preservation sites.

There are a variety of 'sidewalk' types in Kampung Pakualaman. There are sidewalks which are linear and align housing on both sides of the street (Fig. 6.13a). Other types exist along one side of the street (Fig. 6.13b), while some alleyways are not equipped with any sidewalks (Fig. 6.13c). The existing sidewalks in Kampung Pakualaman generally provide a physical cover for underground drainage systems. As such, the sidewalk material is different from the bitumen used for local roads and alleyways, the latter covered with paving blocks. As shown in Fig. 6.13d, there are markers on both sides of the alleyway painted white to distinguish between the public functionalities (Fig. 6.14).

A type of 'waterfront' informal settlement has also developed in Kampung Pakualaman. Kampung Pakualaman extends to the Code River where households

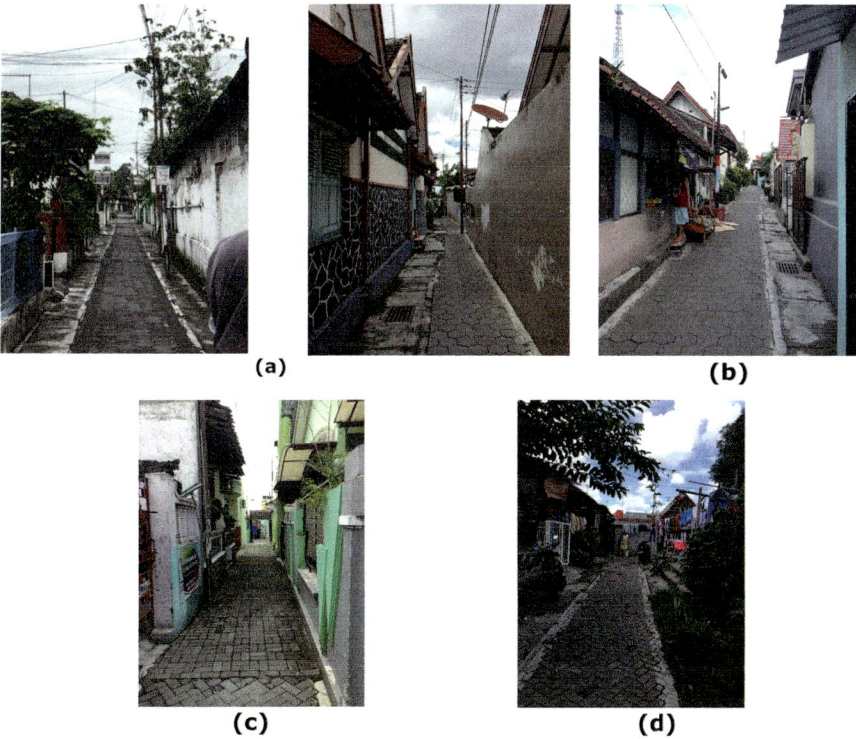

(a)

(b)

(c)

(d)

Fig. 6.13 Various sidewalk types alongside housing in Kampung Pakualaman. *Source* Authors (2021)

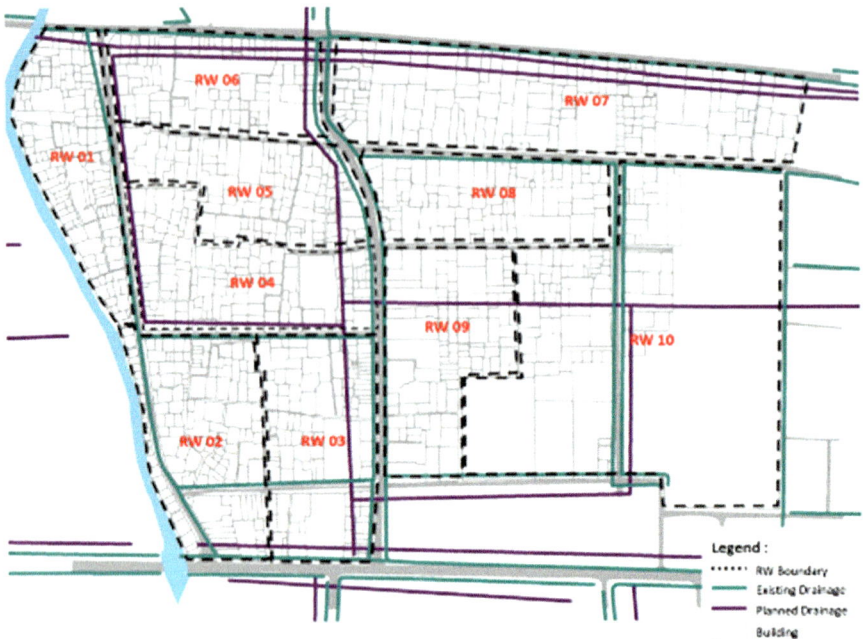

Fig. 6.14 Drainage and sidewalk networks in Kampung Pakualaman. *Source* Household Surveys (2021)

dispose of their wastewater and domestic house waste directly into the water flow. Using the typology framework of Dovey and King (2011), lands used for the water-front informal settlements are often lands considered unsafe for settlement due to flooding, ecological values and natural hazards. These lands are designated as such by the formal planning system in their plans but are highly relevant to the housing needs of the urban disadvantaged when left vacant in strategic urban locations (Jones 2016a). In 2015, the Code River overflowed and flooded due to heavy rainfall in the upper catchment of Mount Merapi. Flooding to varying degrees is an annual event in the Code River during the wet season. The type of waterfront settlements seen lining the Code River in Kampung Pakualaman is typical of the informal settlements in the wet tropical cities of Southeast Asia (Fig. 6.15).

Many inner sections of Kampung Pakualaman known as 'backstages' represent a labyrinth of narrow alleyways. As noted above, Kampung Pakualaman emerged from the segmentation of Kasultanan, with the rulers related to the relatives of the Keraton. Accordingly, the various types of 'backstages' in Kampung Pakualaman are a visible reflection of the location of the original kampung buildings, including those which were separated by alleyways with little or no active public/private interface. Most sections of Kampung Pakualaman are largely 'hidden' from the public gaze of the formal city, which can be seen in Fig. 6.16.

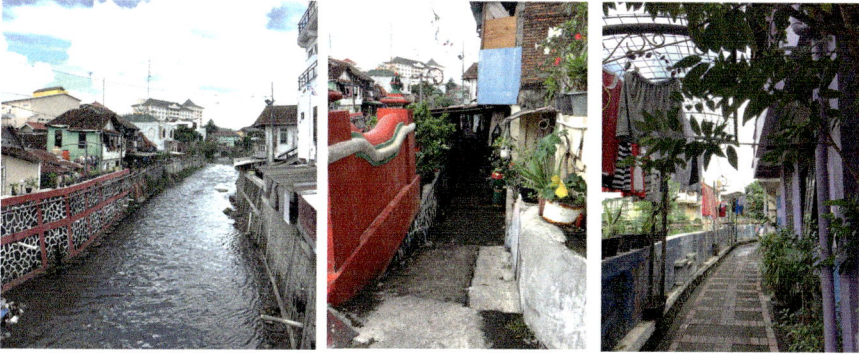

Fig. 6.15 Waterfront settlements in Kampung Pakualaman. *Source* Authors (2021)

Fig. 6.16 The 'backstages' of Kampung Pakualaman. Note the high windows used for light, rather than public gaze and light access. *Source* Authors (2021)

In terms of functional mix, Kampung Pakualaman is primarily residential with a small number of community facilities such as schools, local mosques, and modest healthcare facilities, and the odd hotel interspersed throughout. The 'living/visiting' duality of space and use mix is common in kampungs since residents either connect a shop/stall or *warung* to the front of their private household or construct a shop/stall/*warung* wholly on the ground floor. The household living spaces are combined with these retail uses at the ground level or are moved to the upper floors. The 'living/visiting' combination allows for a direct connection between the public and private areas on the ground level, thus providing options for increased sociality and business trade. According to the household survey and interviews

Fig. 6.17 Functional mix in households is common in Kampung Pakualaman. *Source* Authors (2021)

conducted with local residents, the majority of residents in Kampung Pakualaman work as entrepreneurs (Fig. 6.17), primarily in the culinary and food sectors. Formal activities surrounding Kampung Pakualaman and which provide employment for kampung residents include the 4/5 star-hotels located in *Jalan* Gajah Mada, namely Jambuluwuk Malioboro Hotel and Zest Hotel.

6.5   Interface Typology

A pattern of three primary types of public gaze and visibility characterizing the pubic/private interface can be identified in Kampung Pakualaman. The three primary types are: direct/transparent, direct/opaque and impermeable/blank, noting that these can also occur in combination with each other. The direct/transparent interface facilitates viewing in and out of the dwelling, including through ground floor retail. This type usually consists of an entrance and a transparent shopfront or opening that may be utilized for exchanging products and making purchases without having to enter the living areas of the house. If the shop is connected to other rooms on the ground level, it may also provide a direct visual gaze into and out of the private space into the alleyway, thus increasing alleyway surveillance.

The second form of gaze common in Kampung Pakualaman is the presence of direct/opaque walls. Residences with an opaque ground floor entrance have a direct access way but the visibility into and out of the public and private spaces is restricted by an opaque fence or partial wall. Since visibility is restricted, there is little social or commercial interaction at the household entrance (Kamalipour 2016a). Family members enter via a gate in an opaque wall before proceeding to internal private spaces. The third dominant form of public gaze and visibility seen in Kampung Pakualaman is the impermeable blank walls where no access or gaze is permitted. This type is most common in corner residences where a side wall with no windows or access points defines the boundary fronting an alleyway. These blank walls often define the side non-permeable walls of blocks which form a larger housing cluster.

While diminishing in number, the use of a setback may also be used in both the direct/opaque and direct/transparent gaze and access typologies (Jones 2021b). This transition space sits in front of the residence and behind the legal and/or physical boundary, possibly demarcated with a fence. The front boundary of the setback invariably defines the alleyway alignment at the level of the individual plot. The setback type can exist in multiple configurations from full or partial setback or a combination of both. Like other kampungs where unbuilt private and public space is limited, residents in Kampung Pakualaman multi-use the setback for sociality, mini-stores, motorcycle parking, timber storage, providing stairwells to upper floors, and the of drying clothes. Setbacks are dynamic valuable spaces which might be visible or have restricted gaze and access to the public (Fig. 6.18).

6.6 Strategies of Adaptation

Similar to Kampung Marlina, the adaptation strategies expressed in Kampung Pakualaman have been identified using the analytical frameworks developed by Dovey and Wood (2015), Jones (2021a) and Kamalipour (2016a). The most repetitive physical adaptation undertaken in Kampung Pakualaman are household room and floor additions. These room additions may occur due to a lack of external plot space to develop housing or business needs. Thus, households may add space vertically and/or divide existing rooms. Households increasingly seek to utilize the space leading up to and outside the physical and legal boundaries of their plots, thereby incrementally extending their built space into the public/private interface. This phenomenon has been termed "interface creep" (Jones 2021a, b) and is a key adaptation strategy of households in kampungs (Fig. 6.19a). Usage of temporary space is also gained by placing items in front of the dwelling, such as food carts, chicken coops, pot plants and bird cages (Fig. 6.19b).

The absence of space for greenery also encourages homeowners to create vertical and horizontal gardens on the outside walls of the house (Fig. 6.19c). Other physical adaptations include a roof canopy or overhangs in front of their dwellings to act as

IMPERMEABLE/BLANK   DIRECT/OPAQUE   DIRECT/TRANSPARANT

SETBACK

Fig. 6.18 Types of gaze and visibility interfaces characterizing Kampung Pakualaman. *Source* Authors (2021)

clotheslines (Fig. 6.19d). When no setback is available, residents place their motorcycles in front of and adjacent to their homes. This temporally claims public space whilst acting as a barrier impeding foot traffic and other motorcycle users (Fig. 6.19e). In the absence of formal order for local development or building codes, residents build overhanging balconies above the alleyways. RW leaders indicated many residents will engage with their opposite neighbors on these types of extensions, given the overlooking and privacy issues which arise with these types of additions.

In terms of the flexible and hyperactive public/private interface, two other types of adaptation can be observed at Kampung Pakualaman. The first is the adaptation of an open setback as used for a front yard space by the insertion of an opaque and visually non-porous fence with an access gate at the alleyway boundary. This adaptation is implemented to modify semi-public spaces which are otherwise open to public gaze and visibility into a fully private space. With an increasing kampung population, many residents apply this adaptation for privacy and security reasons. The second common adaptation is modifying an impermeable gaze point or opaque physical connection from the front of the alleyway and dwelling into a direct transparent

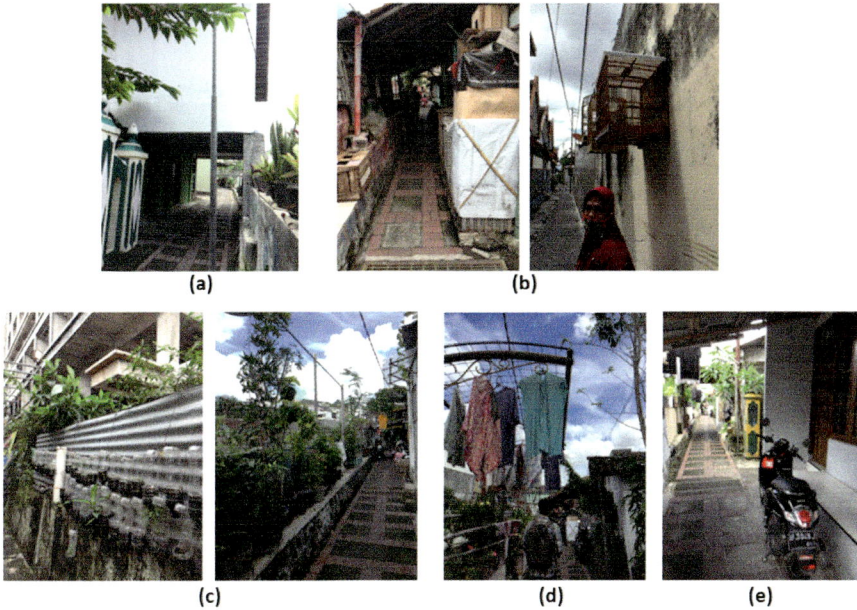

Fig. 6.19 Room additions at Kampung Pakualaman. *Source* Authors (2021)

visual connection in and out of the dwelling. This adaptation is commonly seen in the form of incorporating a mini-store that combines an alleyway, doorway, window and/or internal spaces as locations to exhibit goods for sale to passing pedestrians and motorcycle traffic (Fig. 6.20).

6.7 Conclusion

The case study shows how different planning interventions have influenced and shaped urban development in Indonesian cities. In this context, Kampung Pakualaman expresses long-term urbanization in Indonesia since its initial development in the late 1700s. By utilizing methods of self-organization, Kampung Pakualaman has become a high-density residential area with complete access to urban facilities. Importantly, Kampung Pakualaman has been able to maintain its identity as a traditional kampung settlement.

The urban form and structure of Kampung Pakualaman has developed from a sparse settlement built on an irregular grid, evolving into a compact and high-density settlement. Increasing population and small plots containing large household footprints have led to a tight fine-grain urban form linked by a labyrinth of alleyways. Unlike other kampungs, basic infrastructure in Kampung Pakualaman is well connected to city structure and networks. Similar to our other case studies,

SETBACK ADAPTATION   **IMPERMEABLE TO DIRECT TRANSPARENT
                                  ADAPTATION**

Fig. 6.20 Interface adaptation in Kampung Pakualaman. The left image shows a half permeable fence on both alleyway frontages modified to reduce public gaze by using signage and greening, while the right image shows a window used for a mini-store plus seating as introduced for sociality (right). Both the latter are temporary elements defining the 'fluid' interface. *Source* Authors (2021)

the new millennium has seen an increasing number of new room additions added onto existing dwellings, both vertically and horizontally, with the latter forgoing the semi-private setback space. As demand for space by household members increases and dwellings are being rearranged for varying forms of housing submarkets, the process of 'interface creep' has become a key adaptation tool to acquire additional space on a piecemeal basis.

In Kampung Pakualaman, residents indicated they were happy with the level of community arrangements, attributing this to the long-established self-organization structures now in place to manage different aspects of daily life. The role of local leaders who are called "social leaders" comprising heads of RTs and RWs remained prominent and respected in the community, regardless of changes which occurred in the formal top-down governance structures. RT and RW leaders have obtained a relatively high level of local diplomacy and lobbying skills which are needed to navigate access to different government institutions and their resources as comprising formal governance structures.

Leadership and resident priorities are both crucial, especially during election periods. Local leaders such as RT and RW heads are directly elected by kampung residents, thus reflecting an expression of local democracy which is recognized as legitimate. However, the heads of the Kelurahan are appointed by formal government institutions, indicating that top-down mechanisms in planning and development can co-exist and operate alongside and, in some cases, overlap kampung governance arrangements. Since the local governance structure is ingrained and understood by kampung residents, the heads of formal governance such as the Municipal Government and Kelurahan will need to adjust their communication approaches if they are to co-evolve in meeting and responding to the needs of residents.

Kampung Pakualaman highlights the importance of genuine community engagement in urban planning. This is rooted in the acknowledgment of different governance institutions and their limitations, as built on respect for culture, tradition and religion. Kampung Pakualaman is a reflection not only of a set of organic and complex bottom-up derived urban forms and structures, but also a city within a city with explicitly defined and understood rules (Suhartini and Jones 2020). Kampung Pakualaman shows that self-organization can sustain local urban development and community cohesion over time, with flexible and adaptation mechanisms in place to cope with different needs over time as household composition and requirements change. Yet, as discussed further below, there are limits to kampung sustainability which requires the process of self-organization and self-governance to adjust to ensure kampungs do not 'tip over'.

References

Dovey K, King R (2011) Forms of informality: morphology and visibility of informal settlements. Built Environ 37(1):11–29. Accessed from: https://doi.org/10.2148/benv.37.1.11

Dovey K, Wood S (2015) Public/private urban interfaces: type, adaptation, assemblage. J Urbanism Int Res Placemaking Urban Sustain 8(1):1–16. Accessed from: https://doi.org/10.1080/17549175.2014.891151

Jones P (2016a) The emergence of Pacific urban villages—urbanization trends in the Pacific Islands. Pacific Studies Series, Asian Development Bank (ADB), Manila. Accessed from: https://abd.org/publications/emergence-pacific-urban-villages

Jones P (2021b) Distance and proximity matters: understanding housing transformation through micro-morphology in informal settlements. Int J Hous Pract Spec Ed Informal Housing Pract 21(2):1–27. Accessed from: https://doi.org/10.1080/19491247.2020.1818052

Jones P (2021a) The role of adaptation in changing the micro-morphology of informal settlements. In: Raimo D, Lehmann S, Melis A (eds) Informality through sustainability. Earthscan. pp 180–195

Kamalipour H (2016a) Forms of informality and adaptations in informal settlements. Int J Architectural Res Archnet-IJAR 10(3):60–75. Accessed from: https://doi.org/10.26687/archnet-ijar.v10i3.1094

Suhartini N, Jones P (2019) Urban governance and informal settlements: lessons from the city of Jayapura, Indonesia. The Urban Book Series, Springer Nature, Switzerland

Suhartini S, Jones P (2020) Better understanding self-organizing cities: a typology of order and rules in informal settlements. J Reg City Plann 31(3):237–263. Accessed from: https://doi.org/10.5614/jpwk.2020.31.3.2

Wikipedia (2022) Pakualaman. Accessed from: https://en.wikipedia.org/wiki/Pakualaman

Chapter 7
Kampungs Lebak Siliwangi and Tamansari, Bandung

Abstract This Chapter analyses the nature of self-organization with a strong emphasis on understanding how water supply, waste water and sanitation systems have evolved and are governed in Kampungs Lebak Siliwangi and Tamansari, Bandung. The context of kampung development is assessed, including how the locality was designated as a green belt during the Dutch colonial period. Given their inner-city location, the kampungs are surrounded by major facilities including universities, offices, small scale industries and shopping centers. Uses in the kampungs are diverse and include residential buildings, boarding houses, canteens, laundromats, medical services, and online food delivery outlets, all of which are managed informally by residents and their families. Most household respondents indicated they had obtained legal land status, with more than two-thirds of households acquiring land certificates, followed by those acquiring building usage and rental rights. Water provision in Lebak Siliwangi and Tamansari can be classified under four main types, namely, government-built, self-built, community-built and other party-built services. Sanitation provision is mainly built by individuals and community groups. A key feature of the kampungs is that self-organization activities and processes for basic service and infrastructure provision have evolved and co-evolved with government and other stakeholders.

Keywords Kampungs Lebak Siliwangi and Tamansari · History · Socio-economic · Infrastructure · Water · Sanitation · Adaptation strategies

7.1 History

The case studies explored in this Chapter are the adjoining kampungs of Lebak Siliwangi and Tamansari, located in the northern part of Bandung. The settlements are located alongside the Cikapundung River, and comprise several neighborhood units which lie across the valleys of Tamansari and Cihampelas. Historically, the area was intended to be a green belt for Bandung under what was known as the Karsten Plan during the Dutch colonial period of the early 1930's. Following World War 2, housing and economic activities have grown rapidly replacing the rice paddies which dominated the area in the early twentieth century. Since the settlements are surrounded

© The Author(s), under exclusive license to Springer Nature Switzerland AG 2023   119
N. Suhartini and P. Jones, *Beyond the Informal*, The Urban Book Series,
https://doi.org/10.1007/978-3-031-22239-9_7

by major roads, universities, and small and large retail complex's, Kampungs Lebak Siliwangi and Tamansari have become strategic destinations for migrants to stay since the late 1960s, developing into some of the most populated settlements in Bandung. Accordingly, the residents of the settlements offer a range of affordable housing options and rental spaces for small-scale economy, which have contributed to the rapid growing populations within the settlements (Jones 2017).

The total area of kampungs Lebak Siliwangi and Tamansari is 21.04 ha, comprising 4 RWs (8.33 ha) of Kelurahan Lebak Siliwangi (RWs 5, 6, 7 and 8) and 3 RWs (12.71 ha) of Kelurahan Tamansari (RWs 6, 7 and 15). The total population in 2020 was 9777 persons. Based on the population in Lebak Siliwangi and Tamansari of 4177 and 5600 persons respectively, the population densities are 520 persons/ha and 441 persons/ha respectively (BPS 2017). These figures reflect a population density in these areas of 258 persons/ha in Kelurahan Tamansari and 44 persons/ha in Kelurahan Lebak Siliwangi respectively. Local economic activities in Lebak Siliwangi and Tamansari rely heavily on surrounding major facilities such as universities, offices and shopping centers. The kampungs comprise family dwellings, boarding houses, canteens, laundromats, medical services, shipping, and online food delivery, all of which is managed informally by individuals and families. The local economies in these areas are distinguished in terms of their small scale and ready access and delivery to the local kampung populations. Major activities include home industries which utilize space inside or attached to the dwellings or additional buildings, while other structures such as displays, storage, and tables are made portable and temporal (Jones 2016b).

Given the informal land and building status of these areas, basic urban services have not been the priority of the government (Jones et al. 2018). Major sewage and water structures are those built during the Dutch colonial period and have been maintained by the government as part of city networks, while the remaining infrastructure has been connected and built incrementally by individuals and groups. It was not until late 2015 that based on criteria including population density and the physical quality of the kampungs that the Mayor of Bandung Decree No 648/Kep.286-Distarcip/2015 included Kelurahan Tamansari among the 121 Kelurahans in Bandung totalling 1457.45 ha to be identified as a slum. This entitled Kelurahan Tamansari to be managed by the slum-upgrading program under various 'City without Slums' (Kota Tanpa Kumuh/Kotaku) funding schemes run by the Ministry of Public Works (Kotaku 2020). Many other kampungs including Lebak Siliwangi was classified as a non-slum, thereby rendering the kampungs as ineligible to access these funds. Under the 'City without Slums' scheme, designated slum areas could receive projects that improved housing, local roads, water supply, sanitation, fire protection and open space. Despite the above listing and the ongoing intense kampung development, kampungs Lebak Siliwangi and Tamansari were designated as part of the 'green lungs' for Bandung based on the Bandung City Regional Law 18 of 2011 regarding the Spatial Plans of Bandung City, 2011–2031.

Identification of working rules for basic urban services were based on a typology analysis using current form, structure and physical service and infrastructure assets of Lebak Siliwangi and Tamansari. These results were developed by utilizing a morpho-typological analysis (Suhartini and Jones 2019) based on primary survey methods of detail observations, and conducting household questionnaires and interviews to collect data regarding provision, operation and maintenance of water and sanitation services. Detail observations were aimed at identifying types of service and usage, building structure and design, and signage (Suhartini and Jones 2020), while questionnaires and interviews were used to identify types of payment, time of service, water quality and service arrangements (Intishar et al. 2020). Questionnaires were conducted in both areas involving 104 respondents, while in-depth interviews included representatives from the Community Empowerment Board (*Badan Keswadayaan Masyarakat* or *BKM*) of Kelurahan Lebak Siliwangi and Tamansari, RW leaders, PDAM Tirta Wening (the State-owned water company), and Bandung City Department of Environment and Waste Management (*Dinas Lingkungan Hidup dan Kebersihan Kota Bandung*). The results of the primary surveys were classified and grouped into types of services based on criteria and the spatial distribution of such services. Similarities and differences embedded in each type of service were overlaid with data of spatial distribution and types of governance arrangements to develop narratives regarding planning, operation, maintenance and performance of the services observed. This assisted in identifying the presence and extent of working rules underlying basic service arrangements in the case study.

7.2 Socio-economic Characteristics

Lebak Siliwangi and Tamansari reflect stories of two informal settlements with unique socio-economic characteristics. Despite the broader public perception that the kampungs are illegal settlements, most respondents surveyed had obtained legal land status, with more than two-thirds of households acquiring land certificates. This was followed by residents securing building use rights and rental rights. In Lebak Siliwangi, the number of residents who obtained building usage rights was greater than those in Tamansari, while there was a higher percentage of residents who rented their houses in Tamansari compared to Lebak Siliwangi (see Fig. 7.1).

In terms of land and building occupation, more than 80% of respondents in both areas have lived in their premises for more than 15 years. There were less than 5% of respondents in Lebak Siliwangi and Tamansari who have been living there for 5–10 years, followed by residents who have lived in these areas for less than 5 years (see Fig. 7.2).

Building density is varied in Lebak Siliwangi and Tamansari with the majority of buildings being occupied by one household (53% and 74%), followed by 2 households (33% and 21%), and then up to 3–5 households respectively. Approximately 4% of respondents surveyed in Lebak Siliwangi lived in very dense conditions with more than 5 households in a single premises.

Households in Lebak Siliwangi had a greater number of family members compared to Tamansari with approximately 67% being more than 5 persons, while the latter had 41% comprising fewer than 5 persons in a family (see Figs. 7.3 and 7.4).

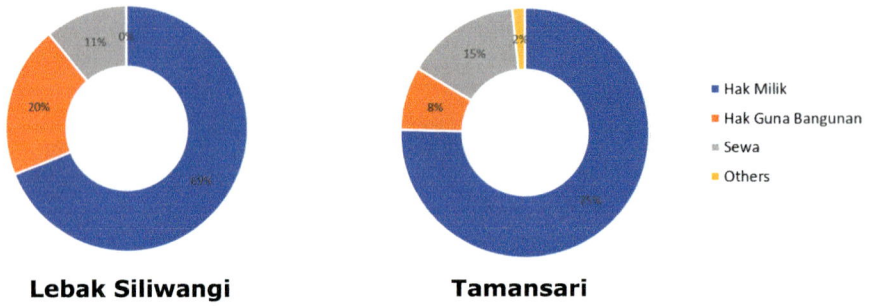

Fig. 7.1 The status of land ownership in Lebak Siliwangi and Tamansari. *Source* Household Surveys (2021)

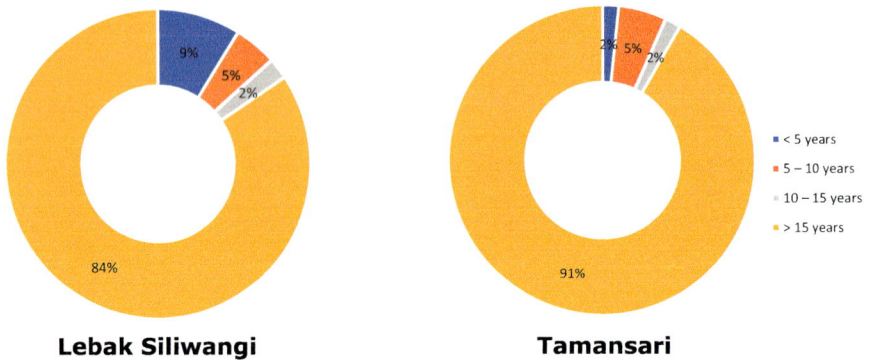

Fig. 7.2 Residents' duration of stay in Lebak Siliwangi and Tamansari. *Source* Household Surveys (2021)

Both figures reflect denser population and buildings in Lebak Siliwangi compared to Tamansari.

Regarding the range of income in both settlements, more than half of the respondents received Rp 1,000,000—Rp 3,000,000 per month, meaning some residents receive less than the West Java provincial 2021 minimum wage of Rp.1,810,350. In Lebak Siliwangi, respondents who a received monthly salary of around Rp 3,000,000—Rp 5,000,000 were slightly lower (15%) than those with an income of more than Rp 5,000,000 (15%). In Tamansari the second largest percentage (28%) of respondents earned a monthly salary between Rp 3,000,000 and Rp 5,000,000.

Notwithstanding the range of low-incomes, there were no significant gaps between the income and expenditure of respondents surveyed as more than 80% of respondents stated that they have balanced income and expenditure flows (see Fig. 7.5). Approximately 10% of total respondents surveyed had more income greater than their

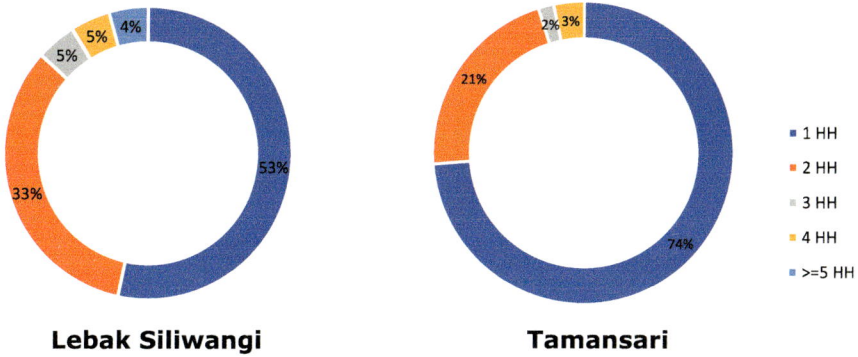

Fig. 7.3 Number of households per premises. *Source* Household Surveys (2021)

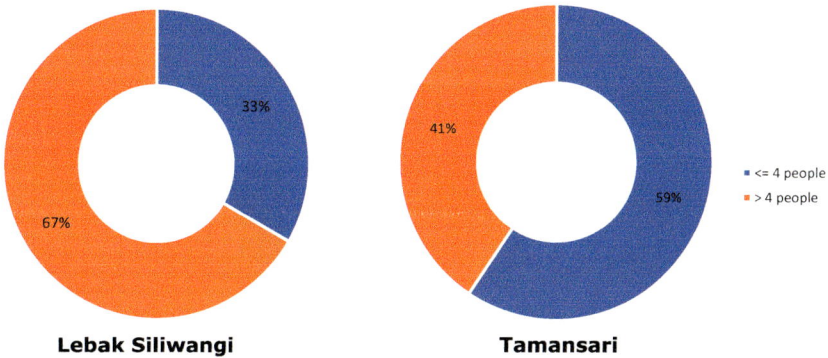

Fig. 7.4 Household size based on number on number of persons. *Source* Household Surveys (2021)

expenditure, followed by a marginal percentage of respondents exceeding expenditure (2% in Lebak Siliwangi and 7% in Tamansari). This response suggests that residents in both settlements successfully manage to fulfil their needs while accessing low incomes (see Fig. 7.6).

7.3 Infrastructure Provision

Water provision in Lebak Siliwangi and Tamansari can be classified under four main types: government-built, self-built, community-built and other party-built services (see Fig. 7.7). PDAM is a state-owned company and accommodates household and communal pipe connections for both areas regardless of their status as illegal according to city spatial plans. These water connections are built on government land (PT KAI and Bandung City Government) thus land ownership certificates are not

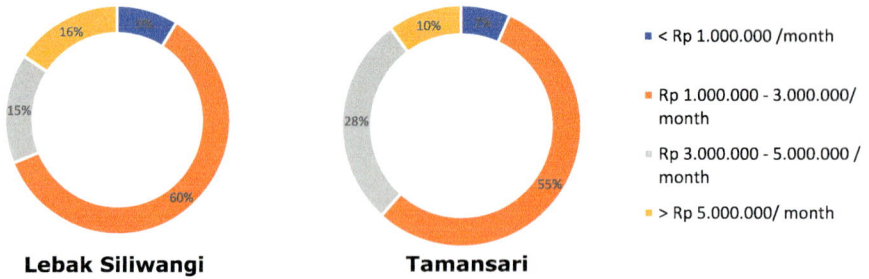

Fig. 7.5 The range of household incomes. *Source* Household Surveys (2021)

sought. New materials are used in the construction which are standardized in terms of design, colors, and connections. These water sources are mainly used for drinking, washing, cooking, and toilet facilities and provide a 24-hour service under PDAM's management.

Since their inclusion in the national Kotaku Program in 2015, Tamansari has received formal intervention with support for the building of public wells. These wells are used by surrounding households for drinking, cooking, washing and for the toilet facilities. Public wells are found in open spaces next to public facilities

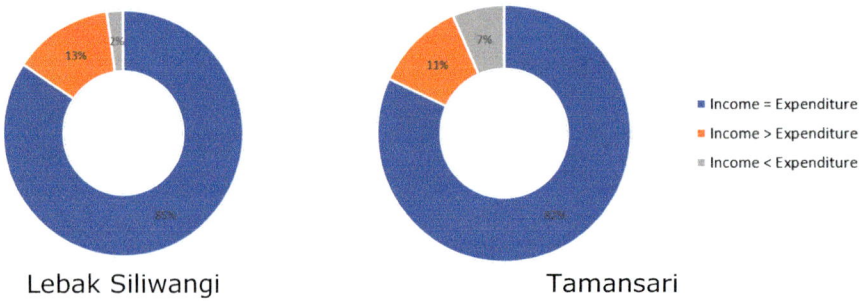

Fig. 7.6 Income and expenditure in Kampungs Lebak Siliwangi and Tamansari. *Source* Household Surveys (2021)

Fig. 7.7 Different types of water provision services available in Kampung Lebak Siliwangi. *Source* Household Surveys (2020)

so residents can easily access water sources using pipes and buckets. Bright paintings and patterned tile colors (white and blue) are applied to the walls to distinguish the facilities from private premises, with a noticeboard containing information regarding projects and community rules. Public wells are operated and maintained by local operators comprising community members. Self-organized water provision mechanisms are more recognized in Lebak Siliwangi. The self-built water services in Tamansari are individual wells, while in Lebak Siliwangi self-built water provisions are also obtained via individual bore-wells, natural springs, and dug-wells. These sources are used for drinking, cooking, washing, and the toilet facilities in Tamansari and mainly for washing and toilet facilities in Lebak Siliwangi.

Issues raised regarding formal water provision provided by PDAM included turbidity (sediment) during the rainy season and irregular flows in the dry season. Residents use temporary water storage units before using water to reduce turbidity (see Fig. 7.8). Furthermore, residents rely on other water sources provided by communal and self-built facilities to fill the gap (Fig. 7.9).

Other issues related to non-government water provision includes unprotected water sources which lead to a low quality of water due to pollution from surrounding septic tanks (Fig. 7.10). Despite these concerns, it is common practice that the residents did not report complaints regarding waterborne diseases in the area.

Fig. 7.8 Types of water provision services in Kampung Tamansari. *Source* Household Surveys (2020)

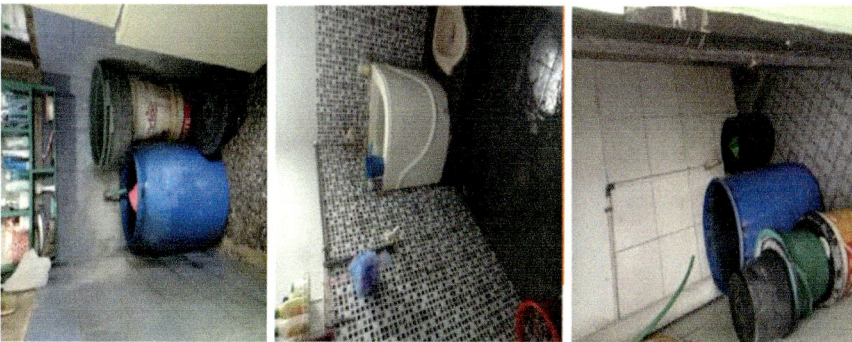

Fig. 7.9 Water storage units used to reduce water turbidity in Kampung Lebak Siliwangi. *Source* Household Surveys (2020)

Fig. 7.10 Unprotected water sources raise issues of water quality and adverse health conditions. *Source* Household Surveys (2020)

In terms of building structure and signage, there are similarities and differences among water facilities in the settlements. For example, water meters and piping built by PDAM has standardized protected water source construction, using a blue or yellow cover to distinguish it from other suppliers, whereas community water provisions are mainly constructed as open unprotected wells using pumps, pulleys or manual bore-wells. Signage is used with both types of facilities; noticeboards or plates inform residents of the registered number or time of service, and the monthly donation amount required to pay for the electricity (Fig. 7.11).

A typology of water provision in Lebak Siliwangi and Tamansari shows a wide range is provided by various stakeholders, such as the state-owned company PDAM, governments, individuals and community groups. On the one hand, the land is claimed by PT KAI and the Bandung City Government, however, based on field surveys, residents in the surveyed area have obtained land certificates and building rights. Water is utilized for drinking, cooking, washing and for the toilet facilities in most areas, unless the residents prefer to use bottled water for drinking. Permanent building structures use new materials for formal water provision with a protected source, while structures built by local communities are constructed with new and recycled materials for both protected and unprotected water sources.

Signage of water facilities, both formal and informal, are similar in terms of design, materials, and included information. Regardless of the status, informal water

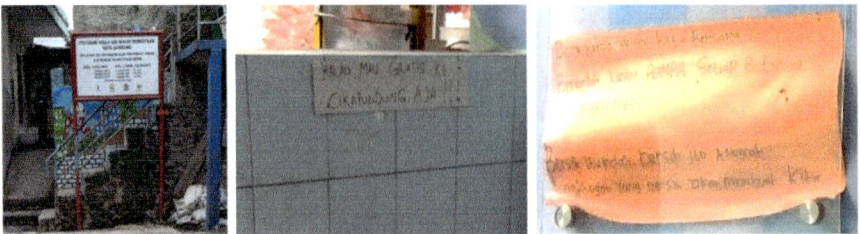

Fig. 7.11 Signage on government-built (left) and community-built (center and right) water facilities. *Source* Household Surveys (2020)

provision resembles formal designs, emphasizing functionality and the efficient use of space and materials. Unlike housing processes which are more adaptive and incremental, provision of water in both settlements have co-evolved through time where formal and informal arrangements have adopted one another's rules and mechanisms. This is demonstrated through the presence of a consistent, structured organization used to build, operate and maintain such services. The summary of the typology of water services is shown in Fig. 7.12.

Sanitation provision in Lebak Siliwangi and Tamansari is mainly built by individuals and community groups, and comprises several types of household, communal and shared public facilities. The government supports sanitation provision in these areas via several funding schemes. Most of residents in RW 15 Tamansari use individual toilets, while RWs 06 and 07 are dominated by those using communal or public toilets. In Lebak Siliwangi, there are more variations on sanitation arrangements.

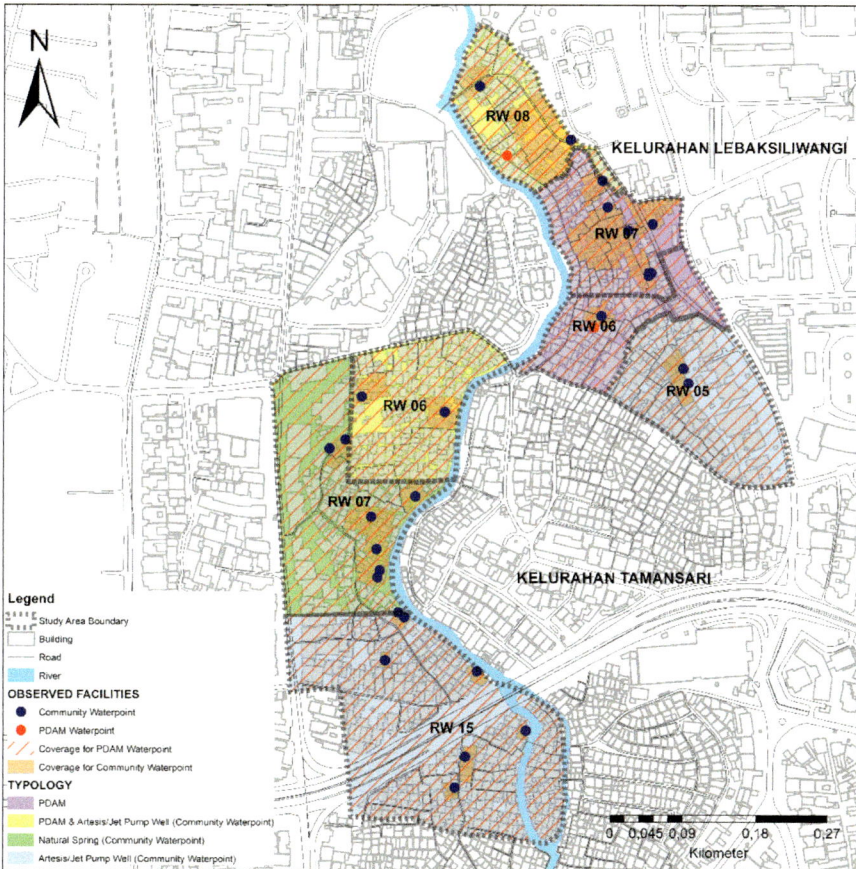

Fig. 7.12 Types of water services in Lebak Siliwangi and Tamansari. *Source* Household Surveys (2020)

Besides the individual toilets within houses, there are also public toilet facilities in RWs 06 and 08, communal toilet facilities and septic tanks in RW 07, and in RW 05 the residents utilize both individual and communal toilet facilities for their daily needs.

Communal sanitation facilities in Lebak Siliwangi are located across several RTs in four RWs, and were observed to be in good condition and well-utilized by the residents (see Fig. 7.13). Several facilities such as those in RW 05, 06 and 07 are funded by the government and international donors, while communal sanitation facilities in RW 07 and 08 are self-funded by local community groups. Residents use these facilities for washing, bathing, and as toilets, with peak hour usage being observed during the mornings and afternoons. There is no fee charged for using these facilities as the water is sourced from adjacent wells or water springs; residents also voluntarily clean the facilities after use. Well-functioning communal facilities compensate for the difficulty of building new individual or communal facilities due to land limitations and building constraints, or the objections of local residents.

The building construction of government and community-built facilities in Lebak Siliwangi are generally permanent and of good quality, with tiled half-walls and floors to meet basic uses for washing, bathing and toilets. Notices are attached or painted onto the wall to advise of details of the program, or for cleaning and payment instructions. Similar paint colors are used (blue, white, yellow) for both types to distinguish them from other surrounding premises (Fig. 7.14).

Fig. 7.13 Types of sanitation provision in Kampung Lebak Siliwangi. *Source* Household Surveys (2020)

Fig. 7.14 Building construction and signage on government-built (left) and community-built (center and right) sanitation facilities in Kampung Lebak Siliwangi. *Source* Household Surveys (2020)

Fig. 7.15 Sanitation provision in Kampung Tamansari. *Source* Household Surveys (2020)

Meanwhile, there are similar types of sanitation provision in Tamansari where residents mainly use individual toilets over the communal facilities. As can be seen in Fig. 7.14. Sanitation facilities include individual and communal toilets as well as communal septic tanks that are in decent to good condition, are functional and regularly utilized by the residents for bathing and washing. Communal sanitation facilities built in this area have a range of capacity at 5–25 HHs to cover the needs of residents in the three RWs observed (Fig. 7.15).

Communal sanitation provision in Tamansari is mainly self-built by the community, except the communal septic tanks built in RW 7 which were installed by the government under the Kotaku Program. In terms of operation and maintenance, several community members act as the operators to pay the water meter and conduct overall maintenance of the facilities. These operators are funded by voluntary donations which are collected from the users.

There is no significant difference between the communal sanitation facilities in terms of building structure and signage regardless of the funder and developers. Both government and community-built facilities include the main structure for water storage/source, partitioned toilets with permanent doors, ceramic tiles covering the half-walls and floor, a shaded space for washing and bathing, and a refuge (direct channels/pipes connecting to the river or septic tanks). Most of the communal facilities have a noticeboard attached to the wall containing information regarding time of service, voluntary cleaning and facility fees, or an information board regarding the program and developers (Figs. 7.16 and 7.17).

The main issues raised during surveys and interviews was the direct discharge of wastewater into Cikapundung River which is performed by most residents living at the riverbanks in addition to the waste contributed to through several communal sanitation facilities (see Fig. 7.18). Conversely, some residents object to the provision of new communal septic tanks connected to the current sanitation facilities due to limited land availability and problems with clogging, cleaning or suction mechanisms. Some wastewater pipes connected to the current septic tanks near riverbanks are not functioning due to lack of maintenance.

In summary, sanitation provision in Lebak Siliwangi and Tamansari represents a wide array in terms of types, coverage, and funding, with various stakeholders involved in their building, operation and maintenance. Sanitation in both settlements

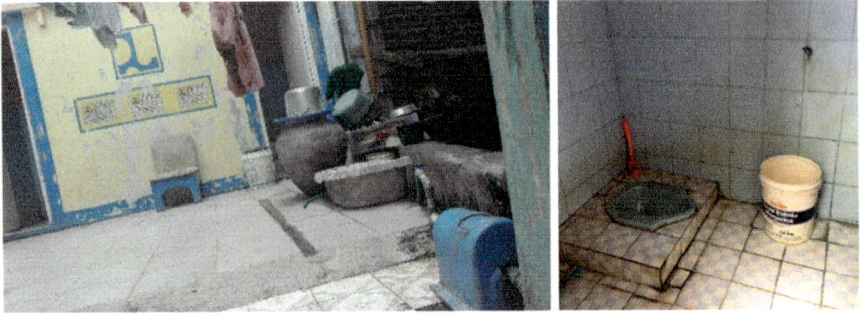

Fig. 7.16 Building structure of government-built (left) and community-built (right) sanitation facilities in Kampung Tamansari. *Source* Household Surveys (2020)

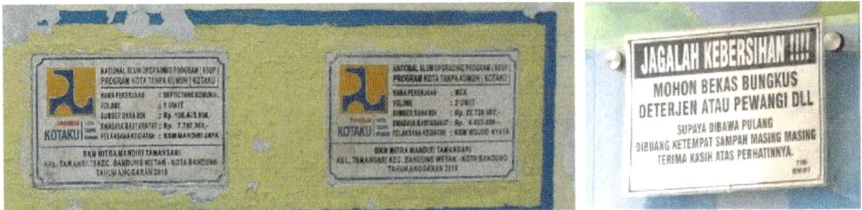

Fig. 7.17 Signage of government-built (left) and community-build (right) sanitation facilities in Kampung Tamansari. *Source* Household Surveys (2020)

Fig. 7.18 Cikapundung River is the main receptacle for grey and black water, while the wastewater pipes (center) is dysfunctional. *Source* Household Surveys (2020)

is mainly self-organized by individuals and community groups so as to meet the basic needs of washing, bathing, and toilet facilities. There are no major differences between the design, building structure and signage used on provisions built by either the government or local communities. Until recently, residents in both settlements used the Cikapundung River as the main refuge site for grey and black water as well as storm water. The details of the different types of sanitation provision in Lebak Siliwangi and Tamansari can be seen in Fig. 7.19.

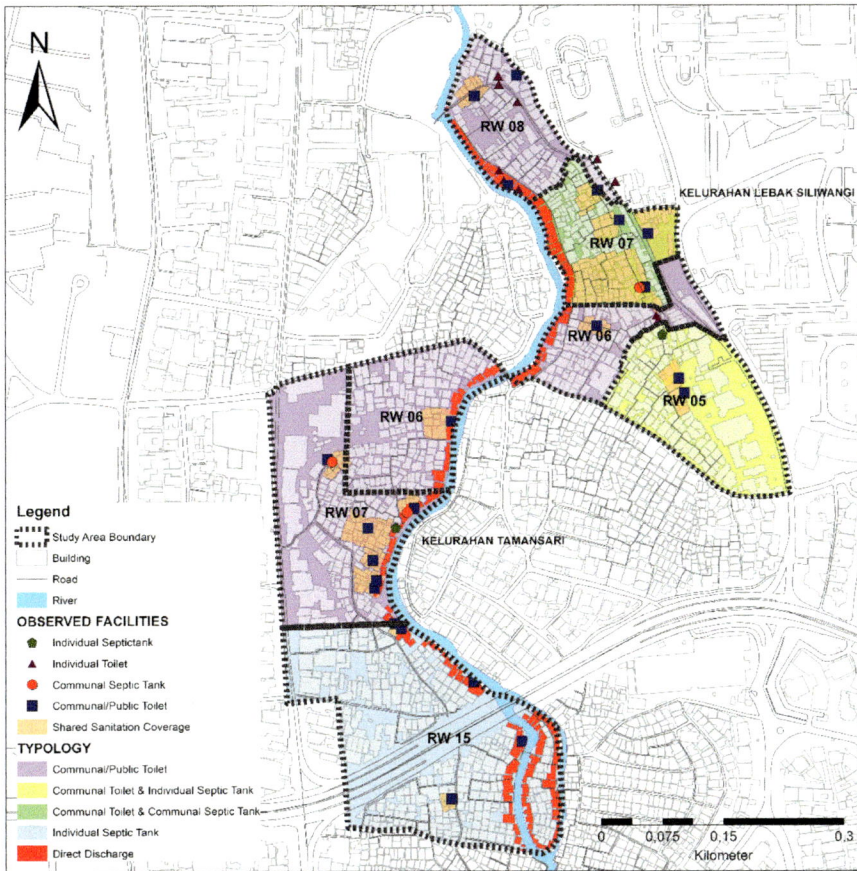

Fig. 7.19 Types of sanitation provision in Kampungs Lebak Siliwangi and Tamansari. *Source* Household Surveys (2020)

7.4 Adaptation Strategies

Leveraging off an irregular morphology, fluid boundaries and compact urban form and structure, the provision of basic urban services in the kampungs of Lebak Siliwangi and Tamansari reflect urban development where formal and informal arrangements have been modified, adapted and adjusted to varying degrees to meet needs. In this case study of Kampungs Tamansari and Lebak Siliwangi, basic urban service provision is not conducted solely through the self-organized arrangements by residents to fulfil their needs, but are complemented and overlaid with services based on policy from government agencies. In other words, regardless of the lack of recognition of some kampungs in city spatial plans, a range of mechanisms working alongside self-organized initiatives do filter down to some kampungs to allow different stakeholders to develop services and improve their local quality of life (Fig. 7.20).

Fig. 7.20 The evolution of infrastructure and service systems in Kampungs Lebak Siliwangi and Tamansari has to deal with complex land tenure arrangements, ad hoc building extensions, irregular morphology and compact form and structure. Formal solutions have to deal with multiple expressions of physical housing individuality. *Source* Authors (2021)

Urban infrastructure arrangements in informal settlements are sufficient in accommodating resident needs to obtain a decent quality of life needed for survival. The case study shows that most of the residents were able to manage their low income—some depending on day-to-day economy—to fulfil their needs, including water and sanitation services. Quality of water and sanitation services were perceived to be adequate by residents as there had been no issues with waterborne diseases reported in the settlements. In fact, residents of Lebak Siliwangi and Tamansari could select different types of water sources in accordance with their needs which enabled them to adjust water consumption and related expenses.

Furthermore, basic urban services in Lebak Siliwangi and Tamansari, irrespective of the initiators, succeeded in providing a wide coverage of essential infrastructure such as access to clean water and basic sanitation throughout the kampungs. Working together, the government, individuals and community acquired sufficient capacity to build basic urban services to function with continuous use. Issues of irregular service of PDAM water became less significant as residents substituted water sources from elsewhere at any time.

There were strong similarities found between facilities provided by the government and communities in relation to building structure, spatial arrangements, functions, signage and quality of service. Both main communal types of water and sanitation were equipped with basic components and structures to allow facilities to function properly. Informal facilities were also marked with a range of signage which resembled those signs used by government agencies and vice versa. This implies processes of co-evolution emerge between formal and informal rules and arrangements whereby basic urban services co-evolve with one another in coherent ways as reflected by strong similarities in terms of design and function (Suhartini and Jones 2020).

Rules in managing basic urban services, whether explicitly shown on the facilities or being implicitly understood through informal discussion and agreement among users and operators, have proven to be effective in maintaining the sustainability of such services. Strong government arrangements are found in formal water provision where PDAM operators conduct monthly ground-checks to monitor and record water usage. Other services either developed by the government or communities are highly dependent on community initiatives to self-organize operations and maintenance systems.

Gaps between formal and informal rules in the case study are shown by the absence of quality control in terms of informal provision as done by PDAM for water and by DLHK for wastewater disposal. Provision of formal basic services is rarely followed through with governmental assistance and training for the community to measure or control the quality based on national and international standards. As a result, alternative proxies are used to define water quality by both providers. As observed in this case study, 'negotiated opaque rules' emerge to assess and improve the performance of basic urban services. They evolve in the kampungs since residents have less access and familiarity with formal measurements of acceptable quality. This includes an absence of government efforts to familiarize residents with such concepts and standards of measurements.

7.5 Conclusion

In contrast to the case studies on kampung Marlina and kampung Pakualaman with their strong emphasis on physical morphology, the case study of kampungs Lebak Siliwangi and Tamansari highlight how different interventions impact on settlement development, especially in regard to understanding the evolution of services and infrastructure with changing housing form. Both kampungs have had access to formal government funding for services and infrastructure, albeit intermittent, with both settlements showing similar trends of development. However, while interacting and evolving with different formal interventions over time, both Lebak Siliwangi and Tamansari have been developed primarily by self-organized arrangements since their initial development which accelerated after World War 2. These arrangements include setting aside family lands for the alignment and width of alleyways, dedi-cating lands for mosques, dealing with the ongoing risks of eviction from high rise upgrading schemes, flood mitigation works, waste collection and disposal, nego-tiating the type and location of formal services, and the evolution of community self-organized governance so as to address public needs.

Basic urban service and infrastructure provision demonstrate a wide range of types, functions and contributions by various stakeholders. An array of formal policy, plus informal mechanisms provide basic urban necessities for communities to survive, with many being self-organized initiatives. Such provisions are managed by various stakeholders so as to fulfil the basic requirements of urban services which vary in terms of design, standards and quality of performance. Importantly, their provision has not been part of a wider integrated plan implemented over time with resources to upgrade living conditions in the kampungs. New ways of service provi-sion evolve to fill the gap provided by existing services, including utilizing available space with adaptive construction whilst maintaining the essential function of each facility. Different types of clean water and sanitation provisions complement and substitute each other in terms of service duration, quality and coverage area. There is no significant difference of service quality between facilities that are built by the government, communities or other parties.

Importantly, rules of basic urban service arrangements in the kampungs reflect co-evolving and parallel processes of formal regulations, standards and procedures and informal values, agreements, and protocols. Residents often agree to follow the service mechanisms put in place even if they know there is no wider maintenance regime to ensure their continuity. The role of the historical development context and drivers of change, plus consensus among users, providers, and operators in defining explicit and implicit rules utilized are important to maintain the sustainability of such provisions at certain periods in time. However, they are rarely sustained over time, hence the physical overlays of multiple systems, with one system replacing the previous system in part or whole.

Like Kampung Marlina and Kampung Pakualaman, governance in the settle-ments has been strongly run by the community members. This includes the key role of the 'social leaders' who are democratically elected by the community to monitor and address aspects of daily life. This includes deliberating on the adverse impacts of self-organized physical and social activities by residents and households as generated by 'interface creep' activities. Often chosen from long-term residents, the 'social leaders' are elected based on their standing and credibility in the commu-nity, including their performance in dealing with land, housing and service issues and disputes amongst residents. They perform an important 'check and balance; mechanism on the myriad self-organization activities and processes happening at the resident, household and community levels (Fig. 7.21).

Fig. 7.21 Set-above activities, such as the insertion of new balconies in Kampung Lebak Siliwangi, are a common dispute amongst residents that can involve mediation by 'social leaders'. *Source* Authors (2021)

References

BPS (2017) Penduduk Kelurahan Lebak Siliwangi, *BPS*. https://bandungkota.bps.go.id

Intishar M et al (2020) Improving access of basic infrastructure in informal settlements of Lebak Siliwangi and Tamansari, Bandung, Indonesia. PL5205 Planning Studio Infrastructure Group Final Report. Institut Teknologi Bandung, Bandung, Indonesia

Jones P (2016b) Unpacking informal urbanism: urban planning and design education in practice. Penerbit ITB Press, Bandung, Indonesia

Jones P (2017) Formalizing the informal: understanding the position of informal settlements and slums in sustainable urbanization policies and strategies in Bandung, Indonesia. J Sustain 9(8):1436. Accessed from: https://doi.org/10.3390/su9081436

Jones P, Maryati S, Suhartini N (2018) The form of the informal—Understanding Lebak Siliwangi, Bandung, Indonesia. Penerbit ITB Press, Bandung, Indonesia

Suhartini N, Jones P (2019) Urban governance and informal settlements: Lessons from the city of Jayapura, Indonesia. The Urban Book Series, Springer Nature, Switzerland

Suhartini S, Jones P (2020) Better understanding self-organizing cities: a typology of order and rules in informal settlements. J Reg City Plan 31(3):237–263. Accessed from: https://doi.org/10.5614/jpwk.2020.31.3.2

Kotaku (2020) Tentang program kota Tanpa Kumuh (Kotaku). Accessed from: http://kotaku.pu.go.id/page/6880/tentang-program-kota-tanpa-kumuh-kotaku

Chapter 8
Beyond the Informal—Better Understanding Self-organization and the Self-organized City

Abstract This Chapter brings together that main themes of the book, arguing to look beyond the simplistic notions of formal and informal in better understanding the city, especially the self-organized city. The focus is on what has been learned from the three case studies in respect of how kampungs are produced and renewed through the concept of self-organization and related notions of complexity, self-help housing, rules, the role of increments, governance and evolution generally. To achieve this, three key themes are addressed. Firstly, what does self-organization look like as expressed in the three types of case studies and their differing contexts. Key self-organized activities and processes such as governance, a typology of rules, infrastructure provision, the role of "interface creep" and incrementalism are highlighted. Secondly, the concept of self-organization is revisited based on learning from how it works and operates in practice in contributing to the dynamics of the city. The case study evidence strongly reinforces that the concept of self-organization is paramount to understanding how cities spontaneously evolve and adapt to changing circumstances. Thirdly, the implications of the kampung model of self-organization for urban planning and design are outlined. This includes addressing omissions in planning and design education (curriculum and pedagogy), and how best to engage sustainability concerns and issues arising from the adverse impacts of kampungs 'tipping over' from unchecked self-organization activities.

Keywords Self-organization · Urban planning · Design · Sustainability · Beyond informality

8.1 Introduction

In this Chapter, we return to the main themes of the book, that is, the nature of self-organization and *Beyond Informality*, arguing the authenticity of kampungs as a genuine vernacular form of emergent urbanism with their own 'different' implicit and nuanced self-organized order. Kampungs emerge as a distinct response to both the historical and current economic and social conditions that govern informal housing production and access to shelter and livelihoods in Indonesia. Rather than being part of the formal-informal binary and conceptualized as being the 'negative' opposite of

© The Author(s), under exclusive license to Springer Nature Switzerland AG 2023   137
N. Suhartini and P. Jones, *Beyond the Informal*, The Urban Book Series,
https://doi.org/10.1007/978-3-031-22239-9_8

formality, kampungs represent a different yet normal reality which challenge main-stream conceptions of informality. Kampungs represent the insertion of chaos into normative conceptions of order, being a phenomenon shaped by a 'deeper and higher order' which is long overdue in being decoded and having their complexity valued. In this context, we argue they are beyond mainstream conceptualizations traditionally associated with informality, providing insightful and rich ways of interpreting and understanding the genesis and key role that informality plays in the city.

In Indonesia, each town and city have a range of housing types through which low-income residents and households can build or expand, purchase, rent or occupy accommodation. Accessibility to the mix of housing submarkets is most reflective in kampungs as they have the greatest capacity to be flexible, adapt and renew themselves so as to fill a gap caused by the inadequacies of the formal system. Through self-organized activities and processes, kampungs facilitate solutions to meet housing, small-scale commercial needs, sociality, governance arrangements and basic services. This allows residents to accomplish their individual and collective goals without the interference of a formal top-down controller. Thus, self-organized activities flourish beyond the realms of simply being classed as informal.

This concluding chapter focuses on what we have learned from the three case studies in respect of how kampungs are produced and renewed through the concept of self-organization and related notions of complexity, self-help housing, rules and order. Also reinforced is the need to explain activities, process and outcomes in terms of context which equates to explaining kampungs in terms of their environment 'as it is'. This includes the multiple dimensions of their assemblage and the interdependence of complex relationships in a historical yet emergent setting. It is important to understand the renewal of each kampung as occurring within a specific socio-cultural construct with its own rationality and language of complexity, order and governance arrangements.

8.2   Self-organization as Expressed in the Case Study Kampungs—A Summary

The ongoing recalibration of the sociality, demographics and the key elements that comprise form and structure of the kampungs, that is, the dwellings, plot sizes, the infrastructure, services and micro-morphology of built and unbuilt space evolve from the needs of residents and respect for local socio-cultural peculiarities. The ongoing emergence of kampungs primarily through a multiple of fine-scale changes at the household level is strongly shaped by the governance, local institutions, social orders and religious rules (such as the alignment in alleyways of mosques to Mecca, where possible, and the separation of prayer rooms for women and men). It cannot be stressed strongly enough that understanding context and changing dynamics are all-important in deconstructing the peculiarities of a 'higher order' as expressed in local forms of self-organization, their processes and unexpected outcomes in kampung place-making processes (Suhartini and Jones 2019).

From the three different case studies with their varying mix of determinants, we see self-organization embedded in all facets of kampung development and processes shaping daily life. These key expressions can be summarized as follows (Figs. 8.1, 8.2, 8.3, 8.4, 8.5, 8.6 and 8.7):

Fig. 8.1 Community consultations are commonly conducted so as to share and understand different issues with various stakeholders. *Source* Authors (2021)

Fig. 8.2 Defined rules in Kampung Lebak Siliwangi are one way of communicating with local residents and through pedestrians. *Source* Authors (2021)

Fig. 8.3 Space restrictions and design of building roofs mean private household water supply tanks have been inserted on an unfinished building roof in Kampung Lebak Siliwangi. Adaptive self-organized solutions reflect different requirements to social and cultural needs, thus reinforcing resident's sense of belonging to their homes. *Source* Authors (2020)

- **Kampung governance**. As strongly reflected in kampungs Marlina, Pakualaman, Lebak Siliwangi and Tamansari, governance arrangements emerge as a complex hybrid of formal state administrative structures (e.g., Kelurahan), locally elected neighborhood representatives (RWs and RTs) and village committees (*dekel*). These institutions serve as a conduit between the district and top-order administration and local political representatives (*preman*). There are many urban actors in both the government and private sectors whose relationships co-evolve in the production, support and consolidation of housing plus socio-economic activities. This all adds to the changing equilibrium of rules, regulations (often contradictory) and the fluidness of order as seen in play in the kampungs.

  Over time, the changing and evolving forms of governance means kampungs are being continually reshaped through interactions, multiple interests, and the socio-economic and power relations of multiple actors, activities and institutional practices. Such nuanced urbanism and importantly the resulting dynamics collectively impact (both positively and negatively) on the way residents, traders and passing pedestrians engage with the new housing forms and adjoining public spaces, including sociability and economic exchange.

Fig. 8.4 Residents self-organize their own waste water systems in Kampung Lebak Siliwangi. These are innovative solutions that should be respected. *Source* Authors (2022)

- **Typology of rules**. A bottom-up typology of rules exists in managing self-organization activities in kampungs Marlina, Pakualaman, Lebak Siliwangi and Tamansari. The case studies reflect the application of two different types of rules which seek to implement an opaque socio-spatial order with a localized underlying logic. These include:

  (i) **Defined rules** are those which are generally clear and explicit in conveying that a certain type of behaviour and activities can be undertaken and is socially acceptable. These rules can be written, publicly exhibited or communicated verbally such as in RT or RW meetings or in the local mosques. They can include visible boundary markers, property numbers, RT and RW entrance signs, noticeboards, and schedules that organize and communicate a certain message or action to be carried out. With defined rules, the opportunity for confusion, misinterpretation and ambiguity is minimized as these rules are assumed to be clearly communicated.

  (ii) **Understood rules** are implicit and potentially more ambiguous. They may be implied in written or verbal communication but most times they are not conveyed using these modes, hence, their definition can be muddy. As seen in all the case studies, understood rules dominate community governance

Setback

Aligned

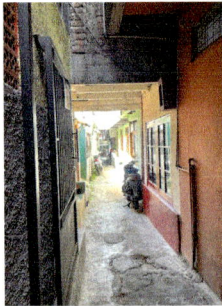 

Set above

Set forward

Fig. 8.5 Primary interface types produced by the ongoing process of "interface creep" in kampungs define the non-geometric alignment of alleyways. *Source* Authors (2021)

Fig. 8.6 "Interface creep" occurs via permanent and non-permanent changes in the alleyways of Kampung Pakualaman. *Source* Authors (2021)

and self-organization and are best reflected in the array of physical actions carried out by residents where they replicate small-scale physical changes undertaken by other residents when adapting their dwellings. Understood rules are effectively protocols and accepted standards that are not directly expressed verbally, in writing or via physical symbols such as signage and yet are embedded as normal behaviour by residents, including RT and RW leaders. They are the accepted mode of organization most visibly expressed in the multiple precedents of physical change embedded in the kampung's built fabric. As a general observation, understood rules tend to be more hyper-adaptable and fluid as seen in the physical behaviour and form in alleyways.

- **Self-organized infrastructure**. The case studies especially kampungs Lebak Siliwangi and Tamansari show infrastructure adapts to the conditions that it encounters. Individual and group initiatives emerge in managing or arranging public infrastructure to complement or fill gaps left by government providers. Piecemeal network extensions, informal household connections, system unreliability and lack of maintenance are the norm. The infrastructure hardware overlaid in kampungs reflect many different physical layers of services introduced, modified and some now made redundant by stakeholders at certain points in time.

Fig. 8.7 Boarding houses in Kampung Lebak Siliwangi are the main housing sub-market that meets the demand for student accommodation generated by nearby universities. *Source* Authors (2022)

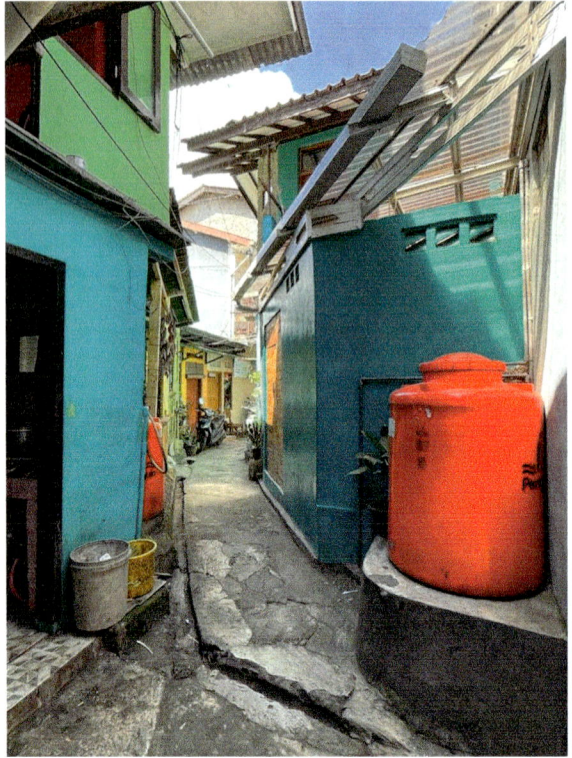

This includes formal schemes by the government and those introduced by NGOs and development banks. While stakeholder's co-evolute in aligning needs, service types and approaches to physical implementation as seen in kampungs Lebak Siliwangi and Tamansari, residents individually and collectively increasingly take the provision of services and infrastructure into their own hands when a basic need must be met.

- **Physical adaptation by 'interface creep'**: All the case studies, namely, kampungs Marlina, Pakualaman, Lebak Siliwangi and Tamansari show that the processes of physical incrementalism are most pronounced in the housing/alleyway interface where self-organization is best expressed in the multiple iterations of alleyway/housing frontage types. This includes modifications to housing setbacks, alignment of buildings to property lines, and the set forward of new building and property lines. Through the process of 'interface creep', four main primary interface types are created, namely, the setback, aligned, set forward and set above (see Fig. 6.15). These are being reshaped and modified in varying combinations through permanent boundary and physical changes through the process of "interface creep", combined with the placement of movable objects such as seating, motorbikes and temporary mini-stores (see Fig. 6.16). Meeting social, economic and physical needs creates an everchanging alleyway alignment.

Internal and exterior built form changes which respond to multi-use demands are the most complex areas of micro-level rehabilitation and renewal. They are created by repeating the same process of interface creep in an ongoing feedback loop. Fractal patterns which display repeatable and self-similar physical manifestations in an irregular form, which arguably represent the existence of other forms of order and regularity, are a hallmark of this process. Such changes to buildings and alleyway alignments often depend on the local socio-cultural bonds amongst the community, demographic homogeneity, local leadership and levels of communication with formal governance. As most pronounced in kampung Lebak Siliwangi and Tamansari, this process also involves querying local conceptions of space, geometry and socio-physical boundaries of development. We argue that the processes and functions which give rise to these man-made functions and processes shaping the emergence of kampungs provide new deeper and different ways of looking at informality beyond standard conceptualizations.

- **Diverse housing sub-markets**. The urban disadvantaged and an increasing middle-class are looking for new ways to house both themselves and meet the shelter needs of newcomers. As strongly seen in kampungs Lebak Siliwangi and Tamansari, for example, the presence of multiple and diverse housing sub-markets reflects the many different strategies used by landowners, existing tenants and groups to access and innovate existing and renovated structures such as a house, apartment, and boarding houses plus the use of undeveloped land in kampungs. The strategies used by landowners and existing tenants are diverse and include renting and leasing rooms and floors, illegally invading/squatting, purchasing, inheritance, plus housing as offered from employers. The kampung case studies offer access to housing which provides benefits in terms of cost, access to labour markets, services, flexible building approaches (both in construction methods and materiality), and supportive community networks that do not exist elsewhere in the city.

- **Micro-morphology and Incrementalism**. In all the case studies, namely, kampung Marlina, Pakualaman, Lebak Siliwangi and Tamansari, the physical means of consolidating and improving shelter to meet resident needs is incremental and small-scale. Change occurs by extending boundaries (such as by the process of 'interface creep'), dividing existing rooms for privacy or sleeping accommodation, adding a floor, inserting a balcony, reducing setbacks to add a new room or to insert external stairs to access upper levels (see Fig. 8.8). These changes by residents typically occur within a set of specific rules and retain the same or similar socio-material and spatial identity. Multiple small-scale increments of varying materiality and functionality and the processes by which they are assembled mean myriad micro-morphological and geometric configurations in kampungs are never the same. Unexpected outcomes are the norm. The arrangement of small-scale increments of physical forms in kampungs as produced by incrementalism create a unique type of 'free-form' micro-morphology reflecting an unconstrained and different self-organized order.

- **Function adapts to form and vice versa**. The three case studies show that rules for form and function change, with manipulation of physical kampung elements

1. Vertical Extension by Adding Floor/s

2. Insertion of External Access Stairs

3. Material Replacement and or New Services

4. Verandah Add-Ons

5. "Attached" Temporary and Mobile Form Elements

6. Horizontal "Interface Creep" of Housing and Plots into Alleyways

Fig. 8.8 Main types of increments in housing adaptation in Kampung Lebak Siliwangi, Bandung. *Source* Authors (2021)

differentiated according to function. For example, in major alleyways in Lebak Siliwangi, two main forms of transport predominate, namely walking and motor-bikes. The physical width of the major alleyway is never reduced to less than 1.5 to 2 m to allow for the passing of motorcycles. However, in minor alleyways such as those in the east–west direction and which follow the gradient of the slope, the alignment has been reduced to walking width only. Mini stores, kiosks and street sellers are innovative in adapting their physical form to ensure their functions are met (see Figs. 6.18, 6.19 and 6.20). This is expressed, for example, in replacement water bottles being delivered via motorcycle or the pushing of hand-held carts. On the other hand, households change and expand their form both horizontally

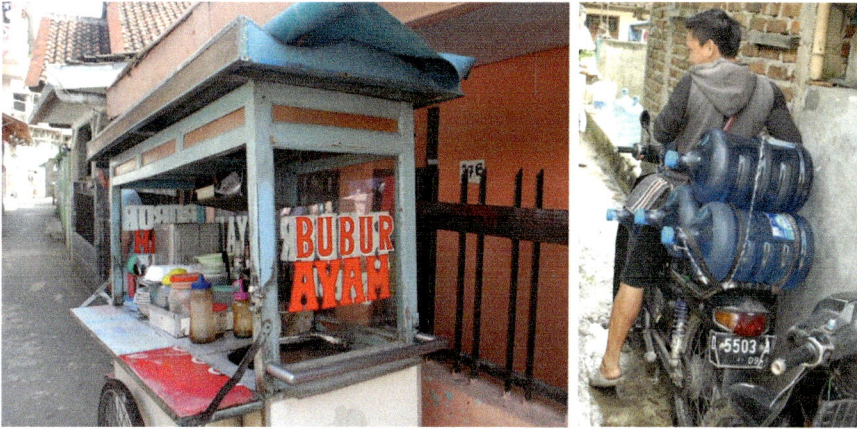

Fig. 8.9 As seen in Kampung Lebak Siliwangi, the carriage of goods and services is provided via different modes of transport which adapt to navigating the physical and spatial constraints and opportunities of alleyways. *Source* Authors (2019) and (2020)

and vertically via "interface creep" so as to meet their functional needs, thus form adapts to function (Fig. 8.9).

As a general rule, economic activity, permanent and temporary, gravitates to the major alleyways where there is greater through pedestrian flow unfettered by the physical constraints of alleyway width and housing change.

8.3 Revisiting the Concept of Self-organization—Learning from Practice

A basic tenet of modern urban planning is the need to provide stability while at the same time facilitating innovation, flexibility and adaptability. Formal rules attempt to bind the city and give certainty based on agreed plans. At the same time, there exists informal ways of planning and shaping built and unbuilt spaces which may or may not work together with formal systems. While city-making in the modern planning era has been emphasized via formal master plans, rules, codes and regulations to guide and regulate urbanization, urban policy makers and planners increasingly acknowledge approaches that recognize the city's complexity, diversity and capacity of residents for self-organization (Silva 2018). In this context, the need to deconstruct the concept of self-organization is paramount as it is the main conduit through which cities spontaneously evolve and adapt to changing circumstances utilizing bottom-up activities and processes (Barros and Sobreira 2002). From this perspective, the concept of self-organization which creates myriad unexpected outcomes is beyond standard conceptualizations of informality, so often tied to negativity. The concept is fundamental to understanding and explaining city development, especially in towns and cities of the Global South where informality is pervasive. It provides us with greater insights as to who really plans and makes the contemporary city, especially the processes, outcomes and 'higher orders' that comprise informality and the informal city.

The processes occurring in kampung Marlina, Pakualaman, Lebak Siliwangi and Tamansari reveal that the self-organization approach to understanding the development of cities is based on the fundamental premise that the social, physical and spatial order of the city is a collective result of multiple interactions. These comprise complex systems and processes driven by many stakeholders reflecting myriad plans and policies spanning the formal and informal dichotomy and top-down and bottom-up approaches. They are part of a complex unpredictable system all influencing and reconfiguring plan content and outcomes at different scales, in varying contexts and with multiple stakeholders pursuing different development agendas (Suhartini and Jones 2020).

All the case studies reflect that an important trait of self-organization is that it occurs through the willpower of residents, households and communities and their governance, institutions and orders without the major intervention and help of a central authority or higher-order controller. The state has limited capacity and at times little interest or desire to control and shape of informal settlements given the key default and important role kampungs play in meeting the diverse housing and other needs of the urban disadvantaged. Table 8.1 summarizes the defining features of self-organization as expressed in kampung Marlina, Pakualaman, Lebak Siliwangi and Tamansari. While the case studies reflect a certain type of kampung that form part of the complex taxonomic classification of thousands of kampungs that characterize Indonesia, the determinants underpinning self-organization arguably exist in varying combinations, strength and priority in other informal settlements.

In the self-organized city, the notion of 'self' as constituting an individual or group becomes the key unit of urban agency shaping physical, spatial and social outcomes. The notion of self in the concept of self-organized cities is inextricably connected to activities and processes emerging and developed at the local and micro-level. It is strongly rooted in local context to meet 'here and now' needs. However, the case studies show that the term 'self' extends further from the central role played by people, households and communities to encompassing the key role played by institutions and governance, such as RTs and RWs, the higher level Kelurahan, City Government and beyond. The informal architecture, morphology and sociality of the kampung must be seen as the result of multiple self-organizing processes and determinants producing many unexpected outcomes.

Through self-organization, what is pronounced is that micro-level parts of the system combine to produce patterns and structure at a human level, with scales both replicated and differentiated across the kampungs. Processes of self-organization, such as for the provision of local infrastructure and private and public spaces, occurs through individuals, households and groups who adapt and adjust their governance, rules and institutions to the conditions they encounter at the human and local scale.

Table 8.1 Defining features of self-organization in Kampungs

Key features	Description
Historical socio-economic drivers and development setting	The system (kampung) and its historical development is highly sensitive to conditions and drivers of growth, including an interplay of livelihoods, land tenure, governance, institutions, landscape and physical setting, and socio-cultural norms/values
Autonomous agents	These comprise individuals, residents, households and community groups who interact locally and undertake independent unconstrained socio-cultural and economic behavior, thus making the dynamics and processes of the system unpredictable
Spatial units	Kampungs comprise spatial units (cells) at scale (such as housing, mosques, unbuilt space, plots of certain size, block patterns etc.) reflecting local interactions and contextualized responses being part of an unpredictable self-organizing complex of (sub) systems. Many reflect the most personalized form of individual and household endeavor
Complexity	The resulting condition from the interaction of the multiple system parts, flows, relationships and interactions which emerge from local rules, regulations and protocols from the bottom-up. The robustness of the complexity of the system parts including fine-grain physical and spatial changes by residents which makes the system difficult to control. The notion of complexity is integral to the concept of complex adaptive systems
Feedback loops	The means by which residents, households, groups and institutions implicitly or explicitly self-regulate, adapt and evolve their rules, regulations, protocols and the 'processes of doing' to better meet their household/kampung needs
Self-governance	Mechanisms of local governance are introduced when there is a shared understanding by autonomous agents to achieve common and mutual goals and processes
Layers of governance	Overlapping mechanisms and systems of making decisions operated and controlled by stakeholders that best suit meeting local resident, household and kampung needs and dynamics at that point in time
Co-evolution	Influence and adaptation of existing and new institutions and stakeholders on each other's evolution so as to best respond and fill gaps to meet local needs at that point in time

(continued)

Table 8.1 (continued)

Key features	Description
Rules and regulations	A set of principles governing conduct within a particular realm of activity/people/institutions. Two main types exist in the kampung case studies: defined and understood. Defined rules can morph into understood rules and vice versa
Use of protocols	A 'language of sociality' and 'ways of doing things' that regulates and directs how rules, regulations and relationships that govern the system are carried out
Temporal dimensions	Use of built and unbuilt space for different functions by different stakeholders and institutions at varying times of the day, week, month or year. Increases the flexibility of space to meet needs and use
Physical diversity and spatial heterogeneity	A product of the culmination of multiple non-linear and independent individual and group decisions using changing local rules, regulations, protocols and processes such as 'interface creep' (as expressed in irregular alleyway alignment, non-geometric incremental additions to dwellings, multiple mini-stores and food carts arranged in diverse physical settings creating spatial patterns)

The specific goals and means of achieving such activities and processes by individuals, households, groups and institutions may or may not be fully articulated and clear when these actions and processes commence.

Unlike the hierarchical approach where the structure and function of plans and policies are decided from above by individuals and institutions, actions and processes shaping self-organization emerge in a relatively spontaneous and flexible manner through local interactions and initiatives. They do not evolve through centrally defined and imposed directions which by their nature do not consider all the local nuanced and contextual permutations that are possible. Organisation at the city and higher-order controller level differs in two main related aspects to self-organization seen in kampungs. Firstly, the outcomes and processes consider a different range of criteria in their plan making. This includes spatial growth directions, land supply, population and housing densities, open space provision, public transport, highways, roads, and network infrastructure for water supply, drainage and sewerage. It is a top-to-bottom hierarchical method of organization. Secondly, their plans and policies generally include an explicit view of settlement needs at the larger scale. This contrasts to the preoccupation of locally driven bottom-up self-organization which satisfies the 'here and now' comprising the priority needs of residents and households to sustain daily living.

In kampungs, it is not surprising that actions required for a common goal emerge in a non-linear and dynamic fashion, being decided, initiated or repeated by residents or the collective social grouping. Self-organization in kampungs emerges as a process and outcome that is an expression of unconstrained individual and group socio-cultural behavior by autonomous agents anchored in local governance and institutional settings. Individuality and expression of physical form needed for survival are extricably linked. Kampungs and their parts are spatial units (cells) reflecting local interactions and contextualized responses being part of unpredictable self-organizing complex adaptive system that have become integral to the urban dynamics and character of Indonesian towns and cities. They are 'living systems' which emerge from many 'bottom-up' individual and collective decisions that cross boundaries and commence at the finest spatial scales. This includes the household and elementary social engagement levels being resident to resident. The latter have been termed autonomous agents and their actions do not conform to any grand vision, only their own local aspirations with or without a common goal (Suhartini and Jones 2019) (Fig. 8.10).

As reflected in the different case studies, this locally-driven process of self-organization where decisions and actions are made in an unconstrained manner means outcomes in kampungs are often unclear, unpredictable and diverse. It is this

Fig. 8.10 Self-organization in Kampung Tamansari is most visibly expressed in resident and household driven 'step by step' changes to housing in the public/private interface in alleyways. *Source* Authors (2022)

commonality of non-linear decisions and processes which is repeated with various outcomes which gives kampungs their unique sense of 'order in the disorder' and define their properties of emergent urbanism (Jones 2019b). At a physical and spatial level, this is reflected in diverse forms of geometry associated with fractal patterns ordered hierarchically across many scales, reflecting highly complex systems within kampungs.

In this context, self-organization in kampung Marlina, Pakualaman, Lebak Siliwangi and Tamansari as expressed through day-to-day life, renewal and rehabilitation is the most personalized form of endeavor by autonomous agents and their governance in creating an everchanging state of informality. Open yet unpredictable complex adaptive systems as expressed by and in kampungs embrace and exhibit the hallmarks of self-organization that collectively create the larger self-organized city, containing diverse cells produced over time and in space. Change is manifested through self-organized micro-scale changes modified by information flows and needs of autonomous agents. This is most visibly expressed in the public/private interface, and the resulting public spaces (alleyways) and built form modifications to households. It is in these spaces and built forms where properties of scalability emerge through repeatable similar or identical physical and spatial actions and processes such as 'interface creep' (Fig. 8.11).

Fig. 8.11 Self-organization occurs at different scales using different materiality in private and public spaces as seen in Kampung Tamansari. *Source* Authors (2020)

We affirm as informed from the case studies that kampungs can be viewed as *Beyond Informality* as they are 'in place' and not 'out of place', challenging existing ways of understanding informality. Kampungs through self-organization are robust and self-regulating, strongly adaptable to permutations and non-linear decisions creating unexpected outcomes. It is the external construction and definition of the term informality by non-kampung residents combined with the lack of appreciation of the deeper sense of order that relegates this unique ground level kampung urbanism to a second-class archetype. Kampungs are *Beyond Informality as* defined by their own ordered systems and rules of self-organization embodied in local socio-cultural norms and values, thus causing obedience to implied and understood protocols and rules. When there is a shared understanding to achieve common goals by autonomous agents in kampungs, self-organization can evolve into both loose and more concrete forms of self-governance (Suhartini and Jones 2019). As autonomous agents, residents and groups self-regulate, adapt and evolve these rules by the 'processes of doing' and feedback, thus allowing the system to learn, improve its knowledge base whilst increasing efficiency. This includes co-evolution and mutual adaptation with local elected governance units such as RTs and RWs where a commonality of goals exists (Silva 2018; Suhartini and Jones 2020).

Through the application of a mix of defined and understood rules, there are certain means of carrying out infinite dwelling changes, and material and social manipulation of private and public spaces that residents understand and accept as normal practice. As seen in kampung Marlina, Pakualaman, Lebak Siliwangi and Tamansari, physical changes are mainly incremental and are not outwardly obvious due to their small scale. Repeatable actions by key stakeholders lead to irregularity of physical elements and spatial patterns displaying self-similar structures throughout the kampungs (fractal patterns) based on an underlying order, logic and varying levels of complexity. The emergent order resulting from the self-organization of the system occurs when system parts find their own equilibrium through the setting of diverse principles, rules and norms by autonomous agents. However, this equilibrium is often temporary and short-lived due to the evolution of 'new' social and economic actions, information and needs of autonomous individuals and collectives that 'adjusts' the existing order.

Changed rules and protocols are generated, yet the same patterns of observable characteristics and properties of system interaction, adaptability, replication and scaling up remain central to the phenomena of self-organization in all three case studies. It is differentiated in each kampung case study by influencing factors such as historical development, topography and landscape, density limits, governance arrangements and social and community capital. Given its role in city development, it has been strongly argued that the concept of self-organization is an essential tool to explain and understand how built form, public spaces, social norms and the wider process of 'informal' placemaking are appropriated and modified in the city (Lehmann 2021). As self-organization occurs without the help of a central authority, people, materiality and locally derived institutions of varying influence combine in random patterns to create unexpected outcomes. This results in informal housing architecture and irregular morphology comprising fine grain built and unbuilt spaces. This process of incremental change introduces not only new power relations, but unexpected dynamics, reinforcing that self-organization is just as much about processes as it is outcomes.

8.4   The Implications of the Kampung Model of Self-organization for Urban Planning and Design

In the new millennium, planning and design education struggles to understand and value the processes of adaptation and emergence that define bottom-up driven kampung development and their contribution of the self-organized and wider city. One key reason for this is that identifying the implications of self-organization for planning practice is a relatively new area of research (Moroni et al. 2019). Another key reason is that the recurrent modernist view of the city ingrained in planning, design and architecture pedagogy is that the city is a machine and rational organism. As argued in the context of this book, it has been the inability to understand what self-organization is, its role and how it can be harnessed in planning and design that has contributed to kampungs being positioned as unplanned, irregular and derogative in city development. This has occurred despite kampungs being the only afford-able housing option for many urban disadvantaged and a growing middle class in Indonesia.

Collectively, the survival of kampungs by different sets of order, rules, regula-tions and adaption strategies suggests a need to rethink the varying approaches to their planning, design and role in overall city development. In flood-prone Jakarta, for example, resettlement was a long-standing approach to kampungs impacted by seasonal flooding and water inundation. However, following strong community oppo-sition over many decades, there are growing efforts to work with residents through land consolidation and safety improvements to make them more livable in current locations (Coalition for Urban Transitions 2021). Across Indonesia, new affordable housing has often been poorly located, pushing the urban disadvantaged to the city edge (Roberts et al. 2019). Thus, there are opportunities for those in position of power and resource allocation to review municipal and city-led renewal in vastly different ways and involve those who are most impacted by development.

At both a global and Indonesian level, the mismatch between top-down state approaches to the provision of shelter and the lived reality of struggling households seeking affordable housing, land tenure and basic services remains a persistent chal-lenge. Informal settlements remain excluded in many cities' development plans, a reflection that urban planning and design is increasingly less interested with notions of complexity, time, resources and community-based approaches required to provide basic infrastructure and services to disadvantaged communities. Translating lessons learned from research to practice has been slow, with global generic policy such as the SDGs and specifically the 'urban' SDG 11 unable to be effectively aligned with national and city drivers of change and policy settings.

Across a variety of contexts and settings, it has been acknowledged that the non-linearity of local contexts shaping informal settlements has not been given enough weight in State-led renewal programs (Huchzermeyer and Misselwitz 2016). Multiple challenges exist for urban policymakers, planners and cognate professions including conceptualizing the city as a system of different system parts with multiple and diverse stakeholders, their orders and parts working in various modalities. This requires deconstructing city complexity including local stakeholder diversity, the political and power dynamics of vested interest groups, local socio-cultural practices, existing institutional arrangements and modes of self-organization and adaptive urbanism shaping cities (Fox 2014).

Moving from viewing kampungs as an object to the subject is central to our narrative of valuing the process of self-organization in meeting the needs of the urban disadvantaged whilst contributing to city development. New ways of understanding city diversity, complexity and emergence are long overdue and continue to be needed if we are to be better in meeting the diverse needs of the city and its inhabitants. Viewing the city from these latter perspectives reinforces two views. Firstly, there is a need to see kampungs as an opportunity and essential to city functionality. Secondly, there is the need for urban planners, designers and policy makers to apply in practice the concepts of self-organization, transformation, complexity and complex adaptive assemblage. The city is first and foremost a complex system, where the parts can only be understood through understanding the city, and the city being more than a collation of parts or subsystems (Barros and Sobreira 2002). As argued in this book, parts such as kampungs are complex systems in themselves and the interrelation between complex subsystems and the overall city is pivotal to understanding the major role that self-organization plays. These are fundamental steps to facilitating a planning system that offers certainty while allowing innovation and flexibility across many levels to meet the needs of all residents, not only some (Silva 2018).

No discussion of self-organization is complete without acknowledging that there exist negative aspects of unchecked self-organization. These are the adverse impacts of resident and household self-organization where micro-scale and system activities do not respect a wider communal public interest. Individual and collective activities such as physical encroachment on alleyways, increasing household footprint, modifying draining lines and noise and waste pollution all impact on the environmental and social condition of the kampung. For some kampungs, place-making has already 'tipped over' in terms of overcrowding, poor sanitation, air quality, drainage, ventilation, levels of sunlight and adverse health impacts (Suhartini and Jones 2019). Location, density, topography, existing level of services (including drainage and flood mitigation), governance, institutional resources (including Government and NGO support) and community willingness (such as owners versus renters, long term versus recent arrivals) all impact on the state of the environmental condition (Fig. 8.12).

Many kampungs that have not 'tipped over' embody the key principles of 'New Urbanism' including high density, walkability, mixed use and minimal or non-existent levels of car ownership (Rukmana 2017). They also display hyperactive

Fig. 8.12 The dire environmental conditions in Kampung Lebak Siliwangi result from unchecked self-organization, thus posing major challenges to sustainability. *Source* Authors

alleyways performing multiple social and economic mixed-use functions. As a result of processes such as 'alleyway creep', kampung alleyways and streets (*gang*) are now too narrow for cars, with residents adapting to walking, using motorcycles, and private (*Gojek*) and public transportation (*Angkot*) to reach their destinations. Traders and hawkers carry goods straddled across their shoulders or on their backs, while others use hand carts and motorcycles to bring in essential services, such as replacement gas and water bottles. In striving to achieve better environmental outcomes, adaptability of form and function and resilience of diverse communities using the tools of self-organization are key principles of urbanity that Indonesian policy makers need to reconsider (Fig. 8.13).

In summary, there are no easy answers to these challenges which also require reassessing the bigger questions and concepts of what sustainable housing and cities should be. However, there are five key elements which would assist in kampung sustainability and addressing the 'how to' questions in improving the condition of kampungs, especially housing. Firstly, coordination by public service providers is essential to address outstanding water, sewerage and community facilities like public toilets, rubbish collection and disposal, drainage and streetlights. Contextualized solutions which respect the kampung 'as it is' so as to better understand community needs is a key starting point. The second element best addressed by RTs and RWs is the problematic issue of appropriate planning and design standards suitable for

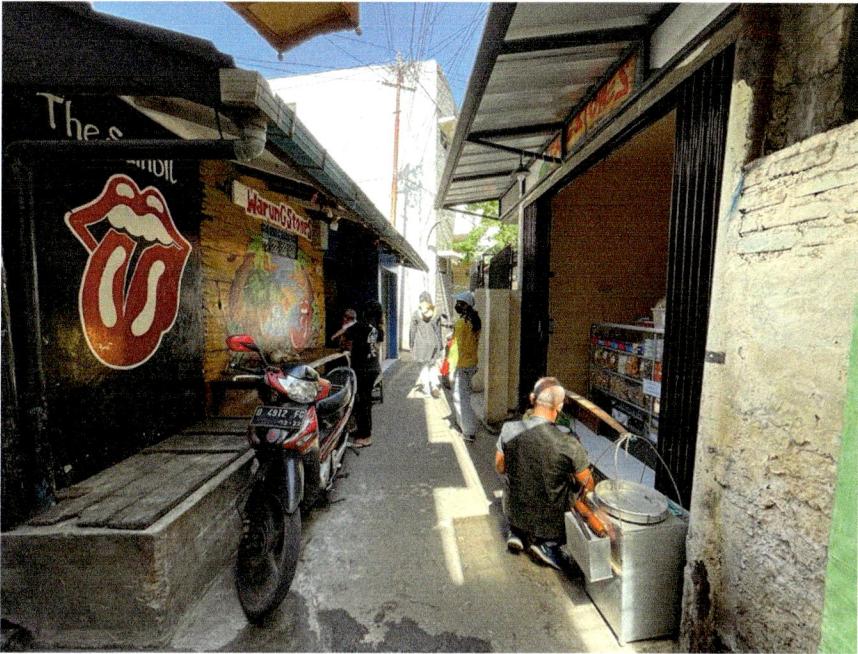

Fig. 8.13 Multi-use functionality of space is a key feature of urbanism in kampungs. *Source* Authors (2022)

informal and self-organized contexts. This requires accepting that certain kampungs require 'different' but not lower levels of services to meet minimum standards. Thus, the way to achieve the minimum or appropriate standards in a self-organization context is fundamental and must be addressed as it is a universal challenge seen in all informal settlements, not just kampungs. Such discussion will include issues of affordability and the existing spatial and physical limitations imposed by irregular layouts and excessive building practices superimposing many layers of services.

The third element is education for kampung dwellers on understanding land tenure and security, boundaries, striving to achieve good building practices and understanding notions, often contested, of what is public interest in a local kampung setting. This includes improving tenure security, canvassing measures to increase sunlight and ventilation and reducing the consequences of overcrowding and vulnerability to flooding and poor drainage. The latter actions will also help in securing access to services whilst emphasizing resident participation and leadership. The fourth element is addressing cost recovery and affordability, including examining local credit measures that can be applied to assist communities. The fifth element is education for all, including policymakers, planners and designers. In this context, it must be strongly acknowledged that the phenomenon of informality cannot be detached from space, urban planning and deeper issues of social inequality, exclusion and poverty.

Planners must embrace new understandings and conceptualizations of what informality represents as part of their planning toolbox (Lehmann 2021). At the same time, planning and design academics need to confront deficiencies in current teaching curriculum and pedagogy given the understanding of notions of informality, the phenomena of informal settlements and embodied concepts of self-organization, complexity and emergent urbanism appear to have 'gone missing' (Jones 2020). The top-down approach currently used to plan and design cities as taught in many western and developing country teaching institutions (such as in Australia, for example) and used in practice is a symptom of the gross simplification and absence of understanding the properties underpinning self-organization and complexity in the city (Dhamo 2021).

The urbanization process in cities of the developing world is often insufficiently planned, being characterized by out-of-date institutions lacking human and technical capacity and with poor interagency coordination. This results in subsystems that are in a constant state of evolution, renewal and emergence often through self-organization activities. The morphological result of complex subsystems is a fragmented set of cells with different urban typologies, yet part of the larger city complex system. As informal settlements comprise parts of this complex system, this creates challenges when formal top-down planning attempts to rationalize development processes and realign residents and communities through the application of 'new and different' planning standards. The absence of such narratives in explaining city planning, development and management of diverse city settings is a poor reflection of the needs of students. This is especially relevant to the mixed cohort of international students now studying in foreign universities in western countries as they will be returning to a developing country setting where informality and informal settlements are entrenched and a normal part of everyday urbanism. Thus, students seek theory, tools and practice examples they can use in their own domestic settings that counterbalance the normative and modernist top-down approaches that apply to only parts of the formal city and its constituents, rather than all (Jones 2020) (Fig. 8.14).

This situation of the status-quo of a constrained planning and design education is a damming indictment of our limited understanding of the contemporary global city 'as it is' given modernist approaches continue to dominate theory and practice on the city 'as it should be' in urban and regional planning curriculum and practice. It is not surprising therefore that when students become practitioners that planning, design and building strategies, rules and regulations remain elitist and orientated to the land, housing and building needs and processes of the middle and upper classes. They do not address the substance of the underlying issues of social equality, inclusiveness and affordability and their impact on the day-to-day needs of the wider city demographic. In this setting, informal settlements play a central role within a complex system in which the parts do explain the whole, but only when viewed from an understanding of the self-organized processes (Barros and Sobreira 2002).

In conclusion, informal settlements are constantly shaping and being shaped by self-organized processes. This creates a complex city system comprising different rather than fragmented patterns embedded in complex subsystems. As seen in the kampung case studies, this phenomenon can be verified across scales. How we

Fig. 8.14 Students from Indonesia and overseas working in a global informal urbanism studio on analyzing patterns of kampung form and structure at ITB University, Bandung. *Source* Authors (2022)

conceptualize and plan the city and its complex subsystems such as kampungs remains an ongoing difficult conversations for many policymakers, planners and designers. A key reason for this is that engaging in such discussion questions the rationale and logic of the 'why and how' of improved planning outcomes by different stakeholders with varying development agendas. As much as new formal policies and plans may want to realign the organic nature of informal settlements such as kampungs and limit the spontaneity of resident's practices, self-organization as a process and outcome to provide self-help housing and modify public and private spaces will continue. The core role of self-organization in shaping and making the city through everyday bottom-up practices must not be undervalued. As suggested in the above discussion, 'entry points' do exist to ensure 'good practice' self-organization can occur, whilst addressing issues inextricably linked to minimizing 'tipping over' and assisting long term kampung and city sustainability.

References

Barros J, Sobreira F (2002) City of Slums: self-organisation across scales. UCL Working Pap Ser Paper 55, June. Accessed from: file:///C:/Users/prjon/Downloads/City_of_Slums_Self-Organisation_across_S.pdf

Coalition for Urban Transition (2021) Siezing Indonesia's urban opportunity. Accessed from: https://coalitionforurbantransitions.org/en/publication/seizing-the-urban-opportunity/seizing-indonesias-urban-opportunity/

Fox S (2014) The political economy of slums: theory and evidence from Sub-Saharan Africa. Development Studies Institute, London School of Economics, Working Paper No. 13

Dhamo S (2021) Understanding emergent urbanism: the case of Tirana, Albania. The Urban Book Series, Springer Nature, Switzerland

Huchzermeyer M, Misselwitz P (2016) Coproducing inclusive cities? Addressing knowledge gaps and conflicting rationalities between self-provisioned housing and state-led housing programmes. Sci Dir Curr Opin Environ Sustain 20:73–79. Accessed from: https://doi.org/10.1016/j.cosust.2016.07.003

Jones P (2019b) Informal settlements and the concept of informal urbanism. In: Maryati S (ed) Understanding the informal city. Institute of Technology Bandung (ITB) University Penerbit Press

Jones P (2020) The case for inclusion of international planning studios in contemporary urban planning pedagogy. J Sustain 11(15). Accessed from: http://dx.doi.org/10.3390/su11154174

Lehmann S (2021) The self-organising city and its modus operandi—informal urbanism and public space. In: Raimo D, Lehmann S, Melis A (eds) Informality through sustainability. Earthscan, pp 129–152

Moroni S, Rauws W, Cozzolini S (2019) Forms of self-organization: urban complexity and planning implications. Urban Analytics City Sci 1–15

Roberts M, Sander F, Tiwari S (2019) Time to act—Realizing Indonesia's urban potential. World Bank Group. Accessed from: file:///C:/Users/prjon/Downloads/9781464813894%20(2).pdf

Rukmana D (2017) Rapid urbanization and the need for sustainable transportation policies in Jakarta. IOP Conf Ser Earth Environ Sci 124. Accessed from: https://iopscience.iop.org/article/10.1088/1755-1315/124/1/012017/pdf

Silva P (2018) Designing urban rules from emergent patterns: co-evolving paths of informal and formal urban systems—the case of Portugal. IOP Conf Ser Earth Environ Sci 158:1–10

Suhartini N, Jones P (2019) Urban governance and informal settlements: lessons from the city of Jayapura, Indonesia. The Urban Book Series, Springer Nature, Switzerland

Suhartini S, Jones P (2020) Better understanding self-organizing cities: a typology of order and rules in informal settlements. J Reg City Plann 31(3):237–263. Accessed from: https://doi.org/10.5614/jpwk.2020.31.3.2

Uncited References

Batty M (2005) Cities and complexity: understanding cities with cellular automata, agent-based models, and fractals. The MIT Press

Gultom A (2018) Kalapa—Jacatra –Batavia—Jakarta: an old city that never gets old. J Archaeol Fine Arts Southeast Asia 2(1– 27). Accessed from: http://dx.doi.org/10.26721/spafajournal.v2i0.173

International Labor Office (1972) Employment, income and equality: a strategy for increasing productivity in Kenya. ILO, Geneva

Kotaku (2020) Tentang program Kota Tanpa Kumuh (Kotaku). Accessed from: http://kotaku.pu.go.
    id/page/6880/tentang-program-kota-tanpa-kumuh-kotaku
World Bank (1993) World Development Report 1993—investing in health 1. Accesseed from:
    https://elibrary.worldbank.org/doi/pdf/10.1596/0-1952-0890-0

Printed by Printforce, United Kingdom